MASTERING
CLASSROOM COMMUNICATION

GOODYEAR EDUCATION SERIES
Theodore W. Hipple, Editor

MASTERING CLASSROOM COMMUNICATION—
What Interaction Analysis Tells the Teacher

DOROTHY GRANT HENNINGS

Kean College of New Jersey

Goodyear Publishing Company, Inc. *Pacific Palisades, California*

Library of Congress Cataloging in Publication Data
Hennings, Dorothy Grant.
    Mastering classroom communication—what interaction
analysis tells the teacher.

    (Goodyear education series)
    Bibliography: p.
    1. Interaction analysis in education.   2. Teacher-
student relationships.   I. Title.
LB1033.H44   371.1'02   74-3722
ISBN 0.87620-551-1 (pbk.)

Current printing (last digit):
10 9 8 7 6 5 4 3 2 1

ISBN: 0-87620-551-1

Library of Congress Catalog Card Number: 74-3722

Y-5511-4

Printed in the United States of America

To My Parents

Foreword

During the past two decades there has been a resurgence of interest in the study of teaching on the part of educational researchers. Equally significant, many educators who are responsible for teacher training have made serious efforts to develop curricula for the preparation of teachers based, at least in part, on the conceptualizations and findings of these researchers. In this volume, Dorothy Hennings makes a major contribution to these efforts.

As the title of her book suggests, Dr. Hennings views classroom teaching as essentially a process of communication. In developing her view of teaching as communicating, she draws on relevant conceptions and findings of contemporary research on teaching. These conceptions and findings are not merely catalogued, but are synthesized into a comprehensive view, persuasively presented, of the teacher's role in classroom communication. The author draws on her personal knowledge of life in classrooms, gained through her own teaching experience and observation of many teachers at work, for many examples to illustrate the basic theoretical notions on which her view of teaching is based.

Teachers (both pre-service and in-service) will find this book an invaluable guide to understanding the role of the teacher in classroom communication. It will be of equal value to administrators, supervisors, and professors of education whose aim is to help teachers gain understanding of, and competence in, their work.

Arno Bellack
Teachers College
Columbia University

Contents

Overview:
Research and Classroom Teaching

The 1960s and 1970s have been periods of significant advance in descriptive
research on the nature of classroom interaction. Armed with audiotaping
and videotaping equipment, educational researchers have gone into classrooms
to collect samples of teacher-student interaction; using category systems to
analyze these firsthand data, the researchers have begun to compile comprehensive descriptions of what teaching is really all about. *Mastering Classroom
Communication* is built on the research procedures, evidence, and conclusions
that these systematic investigators of classroom communication have been
developing. It is an attempt to translate the descriptions of classroom interaction
into practical activities through which the teacher and the teacher-intern can
gain increased competency in communicating with students in classrooms.

Mastering Classroom Communication is designed for use in competency
or field-based education programs or in courses or workshop sessions in
which emphasis goes beyond developing understanding of teaching processes
to developing actual classroom teaching skills. For this reason, each module
provides not only a discussion of basic principles but also observational and
try-out type activities. These activities are an integral part of the book, for
teaching-communication competencies are not gained simply by reading
and thinking about teaching but by studying samples of one's own teaching,
by experimenting with communication techniques, and by working systematically to develop a teaching style that is compatible with one's own personality
and that communicates with students. In this respect, *Mastering Classroom
Communication* is a book both to read and to do.

Advancing technology makes possible this approach. As more teacher
education programs and school districts have audiotaping and videotaping
equipment available for systematic study of teaching, classroom interaction can
be recorded for future consideration. Teachers can hear their own verbal
utterances, see their own nonverbal expressions, hear and see student statements in retrospect. They can use some of the procedures refined by research
investigators to compile descriptions of their own teaching styles and can
use these descriptions as a base for continued development.

Where technology is not available, systematic study is still feasible.
Teachers or teacher-interns can rely on descriptions of their teaching compiled
by colleagues with whom they have paired for analytical study. Then, too,

teachers or teacher-interns can use the analytical systems as a framework for talking about segments of their teaching with a master teacher, a college coordinator, or a principal. Rather than discussions focusing on general principles not founded on research, discussions between teacher-interns and college professors, between teachers and principals can center on components of teaching identified by research; for example, systematic sequencing of questions, the manner in which the teacher reacts, perception of nonverbal student feedback, design of classroom space. The same would be true of college courses in education in which future teachers observe classroom interaction as part of their course activity; the analytical frameworks supplied by investigators can prove a tool useful for looking at what goes on in classrooms and talking about observations.

   Mastering Classroom Communication has three principle foci. Focus One is a general introduction into the nature of communication; based on the assumption that there are certain elements common to communication in all situations, Focus One develops competencies related to communication as it occurs in a variety of social, political, business, and educational settings. Focus Two takes the teacher into the classroom; concerned with the receiving side of the communication process, the modules of Focus Two develop competencies related to the teacher's role as listener. Focus Three turns to the teacher's role as sender; through the modules of Focus Three, the teacher gains increased competency in encoding verbal and nonverbal messages and in designing an environment for learning.

   Although much of the book is based on the growing body of research evidence about teaching, most of the specific examples of teaching cited come from classroom sessions observed on tape or on site by this writer. For this reason, the writer acknowledges the extensive contribution of both the educational scientists and the educational practitioners to the making of this book. Without the work of Arno A. Bellack, Hilda Taba, Ned A. Flanders, Edmund Amidon, Charles Galloway, Barbara M. Grant, Joel Davitz, and in some cases their kind permission to cite their studies, this book could not have been written. Likewise, without the teachers who allowed this writer into their classrooms to look over their shoulders as they taught, *Mastering Classroom Communication* would have lacked the firsthand examples that hopefully will make the descriptions of teaching more meaningful to the reader.

   As always, the writer extends special appreciation to her husband and colleague, George Hennings. His was a contribution of time spent in helping to organize, edit, and proofread; it was a contribution of ideas based on years spent teaching in secondary schools and college. The writer extends appreciation also to her sister and colleague, Barbara Grant, whose original work in nonverbal communication was the spark that began this writer thinking about communication in classrooms. A note of "thank you" goes to Arno Bellack who wrote the foreword and who has been an adviser and friend to this writer for many years.

D.G.H.

THE COMMUNICATION PROCESS

Teachers are intimately involved in the communication process as they interact with students individually and in groups in classrooms; they are continually sending messages to students and receiving the messages that students send to them. Because communication is so central in teaching, to guide classroom interaction effectively, teachers must be masters of the communication process; they must be skilled at sending and receiving messages in a variety of situations.

Module 1 introduces teachers and teacher-interns to an expanded view of communication that includes messages sent through verbal, vocal, physical, and situational stimuli; through the module, teachers build skill in recognizing and describing messages sent by different communication stimuli and in decoding nonverbal feedback. In Module 2, teachers encounter the elements of effective communication—distance control, voice and body control, word control, and situational control. Through this module, readers begin to develop ability to handle distance, words, voice, body, and situational elements more effectively. In Module 3, teachers encounter the barriers to communication: masking behavior, filtering, and wandering. Through the observational guides included in the module, readers build skill in recognizing these barriers as they occur in a variety of situations.

MODULE 1
Expanding our Conception of Communication

Recall in your mind your first job interview. After waiting for more than forty minutes, you were ushered into an inner office. As you entered, Mr. Chisholm—your boss-to-be—extended his hand and said, "I'm Mr. Chisholm." When you had greeted him in turn, he motioned to a chair on the opposite side of his executive-sized, walnut desk. That desk was immaculate—clean blotter, pen in its marble holder, not a paper in sight. Mr. Chisholm was similarly immaculate—navy suit, printed shirt, blue striped tie. He settled down in his tilt-back chair as you took the proffered straight-back. As he directed, "Tell me about yourself and why you want this job," you glanced at the neatly framed diplomas on the wall—Dartmouth and Columbia. Then you began to answer. He smiled, nodding his head encouragingly; he reached down, opened his desk, and pulled out pen and paper. While you spoke, he made a few notes; when he was unclear about a point, he looked at you quizzically, making a silencing gesture with his hand and asking a specific question for clarification. As you re-explained, he nodded to confirm his understanding. When you had given reasons for wanting the position, he leaned back and contemplated his notes for a moment. At that point he began to talk, gesturing with his right hand to emphasize. He spoke slowly and concisely, pausing periodically to think. He described the job opening, his expectations, the hours, the salary. Then he smiled, pushed back his chair, stood up, and came around the desk. You knew he was terminating the conference so you were ready for his outstretched hand. Walking toward the door, he commented, "We will be making a decision about this position by Tuesday of next week. You will be hearing from us then. Good luck!" And you were on your way.

Leaving Mr. Chisholm's office, you thought about the interview. Mr. Chisholm had impressed you as a rather formal, matter-of-fact man. He appeared to react favorably to you. You felt you would get the job.

WAYS WE COMMUNICATE

How had you—the decoder of the messages Chisholm was sending—gained these impressions? Actually from the moment you entered the situation, you were bombarded with numbers of communication stimuli. First, the words that Chisholm used as well as the way he organized words into larger thought patterns conveyed information that you wanted as well as his reaction to that information and to you. His words also communicated something about him; the complexity of his sentence structures and the scope of his vocabulary told you that Dartmouth and Columbia had done their jobs well. But your impression of him came just as much from the way he spoke those words as from the exact words used. The calm firmness and modulation of his voice told you a great deal; and then there was the deliberate slowness that made you know that Chisholm was contemplating seriously as he spoke. Yes, his words told you much; but the tone of his voice, his tempo, his pitch, his loudness communicated almost as much as the spoken words.

Communications specialists consider the words used by a speaker and the manner in which those words are spoken as two facets of a total message encoded by a sender, applying the term *verbal* to the first of these parts—the actual words spoken—and the term *vocal* to the manner in which words are spoken—the volume, rate, tone, pitch, inflections.[1] Discussing considerable research evidence that he and others have amassed, Joel Davitz concludes that there is a relationship between such an active feeling as anger and the way words are spoken. Anger is communicated through blaring timbre, fast rate, high pitch, and loud delivery. Conversely, there is a relationship between such a passive feeling as boredom and slower rate of delivery, lower pitch and amplitude, and more resonant timbre.[2] If Davitz's conclusion is valid, then to fail to

---

1. Gerald Miller, *Speech Communication: A Behavioral Approach* (Indianapolis: Bobbs-Merrill, 1966), p. 73.
2. Joel Davitz (ed.), *The Communication of Emotional Meaning* (New York: McGraw-Hill, 1964), p. 195.

decode vocal stimuli is to overlook some of the emotional content of a message.

Even if listeners are sensitive to the emotional and cognitive meanings carried by verbal and vocal stimuli, they miss much of the message unless they are also receptive to the messages sent through what Julius Fast has termed *body language*.[3] For instance, Chisholm—the hypothetical employer—gestured with his hands, varied his facial expressions, made eye contact with his listener. These and other physical expressions told the listener what the employer thought was important, how he was reacting to the job-seeker, and even when the conference was being terminated; they were such an integral part of the interaction that it would have been impossible for a listener to separate the impressions gained from the messages Chisholm was sending verbally and vocally from those he was sending physically.

Gerald Miller has devised a model that depicts the importance of physical stimuli in carrying a communication between a "source-encoder" and a "receiver-decoder."[4] Note in his model reproduced in part in Figure 1-1 that Miller places physical stimuli in a position equal to that assigned to verbal stimuli. Note also the dots that Miller uses; these dots indicate that though a message is composed of verbal, physical, and vocal stimuli, the message comes across and is sent as a whole.

**Figure 1-1
Physical Stimuli in
Communication (after
Gerald R. Miller)[5]**

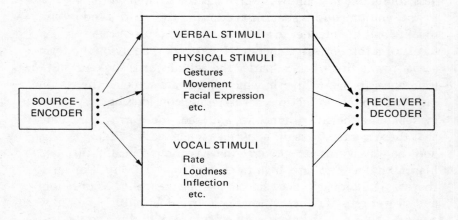

---

3. Julius Fast, *Body Language* (New York: Pocket Books, 1970).

4. Miller, *loc. cit.*

5. Gerald Miller, *Speech Communication: A Behavioral Approach* (Indianapolis: Bobbs-Merrill Company, Inc., 1966), p. 73. Copyright 1966 by Bobbs-Merrill; reprinted by permission of the publisher.

The work of Erving Goffman reported in *The Presentation of Self in Everyday Life* suggests a fourth class of stimuli that operate when an encoder transmits messages to a decoder, stimuli that can be termed *situational* or *environmental.* Situational stimuli relate to the appearance of a speaker and to the setting a speaker designs for interaction. According to Goffman, appearance tells "us of the performer's social statuses" and "whether he is engaging in formal social activity, work, or informal recreation, whether or not he is celebrating a new phase in the season cycle or in his life-cycle." Setting refers to physical layout and furnishings; when under the control of a person, it tells something about how that person views the situation and his role in the situation.[6]

Situational messages also include the way in which a person manipulates time, distance, and things in the situation. Situational stimuli tell something about the kind of relationship that exists between participants in an interaction or about the kind of relationship a participant hopes to achieve; they may suggest differences in social status among participants, the importance a participant assigns to the interaction, and/or the way a participant views others with whom he is interacting. In the case of the hypothetical Mr. Chisholm, it was probably his use of time, space, setting, and appearance— even more than his use of words—that conveyed the message that he was rather formal and important. His office, his attire, his keeping the prospective employee waiting were "speaking" for him.

Miller's model can be modified to reflect the place of situational stimuli in the communication process (see Figure 1-2). Such

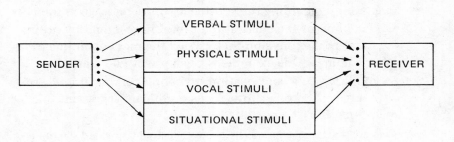

**Figure 1-2
An Expanded Model
of Communication**

a diagram implies how complex the process of sending and receiving messages is; it suggests that to study communication as it occurs in any interaction, we must consider not just the verbal stimuli but

6. Erving Goffman, *The Presentation of Self in Everyday Life* (Garden City, N.Y.: Double-day Anchor Books, 1959), p. 24.

also the vocal, physical, and situational stimuli if there is to be full understanding of what participants in an interaction are "saying." This expanded notion of the communication process hints at how much is involved in mastering classroom communication. To become an effective encoder, the teacher must gain control over the multitude of stimuli he is emitting; to become an effective receiver, the teacher must learn to catch words, vocal effects, physical expressions, and those environmental elements that have communication impact.

What makes effective classroom encoding and decoding more difficult is the fact that participants send and receive messages simultaneously. Even while speakers are actively encoding verbal messages, listeners are not passive. Listeners nonverbally express agreement or disagreement, concern or lack of concern, comprehension or confusion. Perceptive speakers respond to the nonverbal feedback as they speak, modifying their messages. They may stop to re-explain, choose a less sophisticated term, speed up delivery rate, lean forward to convey greater empathy. As speakers function as primary verbal encoders, they are functioning as receivers of continuous, nonverbal feedback. Of course, this is just as true in classrooms as it is in other face-to-face interactions.

Observational and Tryout Activities

1. Watch a television program with the sound turned off. Particularly good for this purpose are the talk shows, the game programs, and the interview shows such as *Face the Nation.* Interpret some of the messages that participants are sending through body language by recording the substance of the message in the left-hand column of the chart at the top of page 7, and by noting the nonverbal expression that carried the message in one of the other columns. One example is given to get you started.

2. As you listen to a conversation, to people talking at a meeting, or to a television talk show, focus on the messages sent through vocal stimuli. Ask yourself:

   What are they telling me vocally about their feelings toward the topic? toward other participants? toward themselves?
   What can I discover about people from the manner in which they speak?

   You may want to record the substance of messages sent vocally on the guide at the bottom of page 7. An example is given to help you begin.

Message Sent Through Body Talk	Specific Physical Expression Used				
	Gesture	*Facial Expression*	*Eye Expression*	*Large Body Motions*	*Stance or Posture*
This is important	Pumped hand up and down	–	–	Leaned toward listener	–

(Tryout Activity 1)

Message Sent Vocally	Specific Vocal Expression Used			
	Tone	*Pitch*	*Rate*	*Loudness*
I am excited	–	high	fast	above average

(Tryout Activity 2)

3.   Study the verbal stimuli emitted by speakers. What clues do their words give about them and their feelings toward the topic? List the specific words, phrases, and sentences a speaker uses that tell you something about each of the following:

the speaker's educational background
the speaker's social status
the role the speaker is playing at that moment
the area of the country where the speaker grew up
how the speaker feels about the topic
how well-versed the speaker is about the topic
how logically his or her thoughts are organized

4.   Become a systematic observer of communication. At a social gathering keep in mind the expanded model of communication given in Figure 1-2. Mentally record examples of messages being sent through each of the communication stimuli. Later record examples of messages sent by one person involved in the interaction; use the recording guide shown below:

SENDER	Verbal Stimuli	RECEIVERS
	Physical Stimuli	
	Vocal Stimuli	
	Situational Stimuli	

Consider the following questions:

a. What kinds of messages were being sent verbally? vocally? physically? situationally?

b. In what ways did messages sent verbally conflict with messages sent nonverbally through vocal, physical, and situational stimuli?

    c. What forms of communication (for example, verbal, physical) played
      a significant role in the interaction?

    d. Did any one participant use nonverbal clues to an extent greater
      than other participants?

    e. Did any one participant use verbal clues more effectively than other
      participants?

5. At a faculty meeting or during a discussion session of a course
   you are taking, do an on-the-spot recording of the communication stimuli present by noting examples of messages directly on
   the chart included in activity 4. Then follow-up by considering
   questions 4a through 4e.

6. Systematically observe nonverbal feedback in an encounter and
   record examples on the following observation guide:

Examples of Nonverbal Feedback Sent to an Active Verbal Speaker	Clues Indicating Whether the Verbal Speaker Responded or Failed to Respond to the Feedback
1. Questioning look on listener's face.	1. Speaker repeated what he had said.
2.	2.
3.	3.

7. In ordinary conversation as you speak verbally, watch for nonverbal stimuli signaling inattention, lack of understanding, disagreement, irritation. On the spot, try to modify your speaking style until you sense a more positive feedback.
8. On several occasions study nonverbal feedback among people conversing. Identify specific examples of nonverbal expressions that may signal the reactions noted on the feedback chart. One example is given to get you started.

Feedback Chart			
Agreement	Nodding head		
Disagreement			
Inattention			
Attention			
Understanding			
Confusion			
Irritation			
Pleasure			
Desire to speak			
Desire to listen			

9. Experiment with nonverbal feedback to determine its effect on a speaker. Show agreement overtly through facial expressions, eye expressions, gestures. How does this affect the speaker? Later send overt feedback signaling disagreement. Try the same with comprehension/confusion; inattention/attention; boredom/ interest. Experiment with a "dead pan" expression. How does that affect a speaker?

10. Identify nonverbal stimuli we use to communicate specific verbal messages. One example is given on the following chart. Remember that an expression can have any number of different meanings depending on the context.

Verbal Expression	Nonverbal Expression of the Message
a. I like you.	Smiling warmly; patting on the back; kissing.
b. Not now.	
c. Come here.	
d. I am in a hurry.	
e. That is terrible.	
f. I feel important.	
g. Hello.	

11. Study a person's appearance and draw inferences based on your observations.

    a. *Description of a person's appearance:*

    b. *Inferences you may draw:*
      whether the person is engaging in formal social activity, work, or informal recreation
      what social status the person holds or wants to hold
      whether the person perceives himself as a child, a youth, an energetic young adult, a mature middle-aged person, a senior citizen
      whether the person is physically preparing for spring, summer, fall, winter

12. Study a setting—the physical layout and furnishings. Describe the setting and draw inferences about the expectations of the person who designed that setting.

    a. *Description of the setting:*

    b. *Inferences you may draw:*
      how the designer of the setting (the office, classroom, living room) views the interaction that will occur there
      how the designer views his role in the situation
      how the designer views relationships among participants in the situation

13. Write a description of an encounter in which you tell what was "said" both verbally and nonverbally. Use the Chisholm example at the beginning of the module as a guide for things to include in your description.

MODULE 2
Encountering the Elements of Effective Communication

MODULE GOALS

The teacher gains competency in—

recognizing messages sent by distance and using distance to send messages

speaking with vocal and physical expressiveness

using words clearly, with understanding of the possible connotations words carry and with understanding that verbal style must change as audience changes

controlling the situational messages he sends

One summer I observed two classes at Columbia Teachers College. The first, in children's literature, was taught by Leland Jacobs. From the moment Jake walked into the room until the moment his august presence disappeared down the hall, he held his listeners spellbound. He brought smiles to faces as he talked about the boy in *Backward Day* who spent a day doing everything backward; he made his listeners empathize with Peter Rabbit as Peter explored Mr. McGregor's carrot patch; he stimulated his listeners intellectually as he discussed relationships between picture and word in picture-story books. His was a full-frequency delivery.

After an hour with Jake, I went on to a second class, the subject matter of which had the potential to be as fascinating as children's literature. It was not! The professor droned on, casting no spell other than sleepiness, arousing no emotion other than exasperation, and stimulating few exciting thoughts. His was a flaccid delivery.

What makes the difference between a flaccid and a full-frequency delivery? Let us consider four elements that make a difference: distance control, body and vocal control, word control, and situational control.

DISTANCE CONTROL

A speaker—whether a conversationalist talking across the dinner table or a teacher working with a group of students—is attempting to build a relationship with other participants. One way to build a relationship is through manipulation of the distance maintained

13

between the speaker and other participants. The dinner guest may lean the body or move an arm toward another person to indicate a higher level of personal involvement. In American social situations, the conversationalist may bring a chair closer to a companion's or move objects lying in the path between them. The person interacting with a larger group uses many of the same techniques—leaning toward, gesturing toward, moving toward. If standing, a speaker manipulates bigger distances—even walking across an entire room; the walking suggests "I want to make closer contact with you." The speaker is able to walk around furniture so that no physical obstacles separate him from other participants; distance can be covered rapidly or slowly, the speed communicating level of interest in being close.

That manipulating distance can serve as a means of defining a relationship and of making greater personal contact arises from the fact that man's physical boundary does not begin and end with the skin and from the fact that the distance we maintain between our- selves and others has inherent communication value.[1] Edward T. Hall proposes that man is encapsulated within a series of concentric space bubbles. The first of these bubbles, or *intimate space* as Hall calls it, extends out from the individual for about 18 inches.[2] Typically, Americans feel a sense of discomfort when a stranger intrudes upon their intimate space; they may stiffen muscles in reaction, as on a crowded elevator. For this reason, venturing into someone's intimate space implies something about the emotional closeness of the relationship people feel they have or desire to have.

Loved ones are allowed to enter one's intimate space; those who are perceived in a serving role have access as well. Dentists, doctors, nurses, teachers, sales people in the garment trade—all can enter one's intimate space with impunity. In a sense, one would be surprised if these practitioners failed to move close to perform their work.

Hall uses Hediger's term *personal distance* for the area between 18 inches and 4 feet. Within this range, physical contact by touching is still possible; the fine detail of the other's body and dress is per- ceptible; and people typically moderate the loudness of voice. Con- versations carried on at this distance give participants a heightened sense of sharing than conversations pursued at greater distances.

---

1. Edward T. Hall, *The Hidden Dimension* (Garden City, N.Y.: Doubleday, 1966), p. 108.
2. *Ibid.*, p. 110.

Personal distance is generally reserved for friends and family members.[3]

Social distance is the space between 4 and 12 feet; it is the distance at which interaction between coworkers as well as formal business and social discourse generally occur. At this distance, the chance of touching is less, some of the detail of others' body and dress is lost, and the need for eye contact is increased.[4]

The area beyond 12 feet blends into what Hall calls *public distance.* Hall concludes that interaction assumes a more formal character when participants are separated by larger distances: "...a more careful choice of words and phrasing of sentences as well as grammatical or syntactic shifts occur at this distance." Fine details of clothes and body as well as the specific look of the other's eyes—color, clarity, tension—are imperceptible. A person communicating across public distance gets only limited nonverbal feedback as a result. Even nuances of tone and voice quality may be lost; communicating across 12 or more feet, the voice must be raised and words clearly enunciated. The result is a lowered sense of involvement.[5]

Failure to use distance productively accounts for some speakers' inability to communicate effectively. For instance, the ineffectual speaker described earlier in the module positioned himself on a raised platform, behind a lectern, and at a considerable distance from the first row of students. He was maintaining public distance without employing any of the exaggerated gestures and definitive eye contact necessary to build a relationship across that distance. Furthermore, he failed to vary distance to emphasize or to change the formality of the class.

In contrast, Professor Jacobs used no lectern or platform. He positioned himself between 3 and 8 feet from the front row of students and moved across the room and up the center aisle to communicate more directly. As he approached, he lowered his voice and leaned forward as if to suggest a special significance. When he chose to make a point in striking fashion, he moved away, raising his voice and shifting to formal verbal style. Here he was using distance to achieve not only emphasis and variety but also a sense of personal contact.

---

3. *Ibid.*, p. 112.
4. *Ibid.*, p. 114.
5. *Ibid.*, p. 116.

Distance obviously communicates in situations other than the lecture setting. Failure to enter the personal zone of another when the job to be done demands closeness speaks significantly; a drawing away from body contact sends a similar message. The pulling together of chairs to form a discussion group may nonverbally set the stage for cooperative activity; the action literally says, "We are coming together." The same message is sent by a teacher who draws a chair up to a student's and leans into the student's personal space to give individualized assistance with a difficult task and by a worker who leans an arm companionably against the desk on which a coworker rests an arm. Each is exchanging social or formal distance for personal distance and sending a message in the process.

Encounters with Distance

1. Deliberately move into the personal space of someone whom you know only slightly. Watch his reactions. Julius Fast describes an experiment carried out by a psychologist in which the psychologist moved his own knife, fork, plate, glass . . . across the table into the "territory" of a friend with whom he was eating. You may want to try that experiment also and observe the reaction of the person into whose territory you have moved.

2. Try the opposite experiment. Rather than selecting a chair close by a person with whom you are chatting, sit at a distance. How does that affect conversation?

3. Watch adults as they interact. What kinds of conclusions can you draw about the closeness of the relationship shared, based on the distance they maintain between one another and the amount of physical contact that occurs?

4. Observe the distances children maintain between one another and the amount of physical contact they make. Do they seem to need more or less distance between one another than adults need? Do you as teacher tend to interact with students at a closer distance than you would with adults?

5. In interactions that occur in a variety of situations, focus on the distance people maintain and make note of instances in which intimate, personal, social, and public distances were used. Record specific instances of use of each kind of distance on the following chart, and then draw some conclusions about the general ways people use distance in interaction.

INTIMATE DISTANCE	PERSONAL DISTANCE
SOCIAL DISTANCE	FORMAL DISTANCE

6. Watch how you use distance in interactions. Do you tend to move in close or to keep your distance? Try varying your typical pattern to see if you can use distance more effectively.

VOICE AND BODY CONTROL

A reciprocal of distance is loudness or strength of voice. As we move closer together, we tend to lower our voices, whereas when we communicate at formal distances, we project more forcefully. Failure to moderate voice level as distance diminishes may make our words less effective.

Pitch has a comparable effect. The high-pitched voice can grate on a decoder's nerves so that the listener turns off to the words spoken; the very deep voice can distract from the message. Conversely, assisted by variations in loudness, changes in pitch can create a mood that can be the message in and of itself.

Speed of delivery carries impact as well. Sometimes when a task must be completed with dispatch, the encoder speaks quickly with a clip to the voice that adds "Let's not fiddle around." In contrast, words spoken slowly can communicate a sense of leisureliness or, under different conditions, careful consideration of an idea. Of course, speed of delivery has an effect on the listener's ability to receive. When words are rushed, the message may be lost; when words come too slowly, attention may wander.

The speaker who does not vary pitch, loudness, and rate courts monotony and fails to use the emotional potential of the voice. Diversity keeps people awake, adds animation, and indicates to a listener what the encoder believes is important. When a speaker lowers his voice suddenly, listeners are forced to adjust their focus; words delivered forcefully after several almost whispered sentences may restore attention.

Pitch, loudness, and rate of delivery also convey emotional meanings. Excited or enthused, a speaker says so by raising the loudness and pitch of his voice. Unimpressed or disinterested, he communicates his feelings by an evenness of pitch. As Harriett Grim notes in *Practical Voice Training*, "excitement, joy, eagerness, and flashing anger are a few of the moods and attitudes expressed by rapid rates. Reverence, sorrow, wonder, awe, and dignified thinking" are reflected through slow tempo.[6]

Grim's conclusions are supported by research concerned with vocal expression of emotion. Summarizing studies completed through 1961, Davitz writes: "Regardless of the technique used, all studies of adults thus far reported in the literature agree that emotional meanings can be communicated accurately by vocal expression."[7] Investigating children's ability to identify emotional expressions, Dimitrovsky reports that children between the ages of five and twelve show "a gradual and steadily progressive increase in the ability to identify emotional meaning of vocal expressions." She also reports that individual differences in this ability are as striking among children as they are among adults.[8]

Vocal expression of emotion is related also to tone of voice. Spoken words may be innocuous; written on a page, they would not

6. Harriet Grim, *Practical Voice Training* (New York: Appleton-Century-Crofts, 1948), p. 29.
7. Joel Davitz, *The Communication of Emotional Meaning* (New York: McGraw-Hill, 1969), p. 23.
8. Lilly Dimitrovsky, "The Ability to Identify Emotional Expressions at Successive Levels," in Joel Davitz (ed.), *The Communication of Emotional Meaning* (New York: McGraw-Hill, 1964), pp. 81-82.

cause offense. Tone makes the difference. Tone can communicate approval or disapproval, determination or indecisiveness, command of the situation or fear; for words can be delivered sarcastically, respectfully, threateningly, lovingly, crisply. Interestingly enough, as the research procedures of Davitz and others indicate, a speaker need not actually feel an emotion to communicate it vocally. Encoders can speak *as if* they are angry or *as if* they are happy and communicate that feeling to decoders.[9]

Body language complements the emotional meanings sent vocally. "Body and mind are so closely linked that an idea vividly experienced not only prompts speech but gesture also." In their book *Oral Communication*, Donald Bryant and Karl Wallace go on to suggest that body language is not an invention that speakers deliberately plant here and there as they speak; the motions of the body must be genuine and spontaneous to be effective. Genuineness and spontaneity come when the body is *"free to respond* to the meanings of the mind." Speakers must handle themselves in ways that will not inhibit the natural bodily responses that accompany verbal expression of thought. They must learn to relax with the body so that motions are smooth and the body responds freely and easily.[10]

One emotion that body language reveals is insecurity. Take, for instance, what a student teacher going into a classroom for the first time tells students physically. The student teacher may have a lesson plan that is organizationally sound, may have a thorough understanding of subject-matter content, and may have an extensive understanding of children. But the lesson just doesn't go over. One reason may be insecurity communicated by tone of voice and hesitant body language. The student teacher has not yet perceived himself as the person in charge. The beginner looks toward the cooperating teacher in a way that asks, "Is it OK to do this?" He holds back physically before moving into a disciplinary role, pauses an instant too long before going on to the next item, or holds his chin indecisively. All these motions are being "read" by the students in the class. They conclude, "The teacher isn't sure," and may take advantage of the new teacher's insecurity.

Through body language too we send messages that are basic to the logistics of communication. According to Kenneth Strongman of the University of Exeter, England, typically a speaker looks away

9. Davitz, *op. cit.*, p. 189.
10. Donald Bryant and Karl Wallace, *Oral Communication: A Short Course in Speaking*, 3rd ed. (New York: Appleton-Century-Crofts, 1962), p. 140.

when beginning to talk whereas a listener keeps eyes focused on the active speaker.[11] Typically also the active speaker looks away when pausing only momentarily to think; looking away signals an intention to continue speaking verbally. On the other hand, when a speaker intends to stop talking his eyes return to those of the listener to ask, "What do you think?" In this way, listeners know when it is their turn to speak verbally while active speakers get some feedback from the look in the listeners' eyes.

Body language sends cognitive as well as logistical and emotional meanings. Gestures may describe, as when the hands are used to indicate spherical shape; they may tell where as when a finger points in a direction; they may contrast and compare; they may say, "This is important," as when a speaker nods while speaking a specific word; they may gain attention as when someone raps on the table to tell others to attend.[12] In each of these instances factual information is communicated physically.

What has been said so far makes obvious the fact that failure to realize the potential of voice and body can limit the effectiveness of communication. The result may be a flaccid delivery lacking in highs and lows, in emphasis, in variety. Tone of voice may remain static; few gestures may be employed to emphasize and clarify; facial expressions may be nonexpressive; and pauses, changes in tempo, and fluctuations in pitch may be unrelated to the verbal message. In reaction, the listener ceases to attend and may adopt waiting behavior.

A second result may be a conflict between the verbal and physical messages—what psychologists call *double-bind communication*.[13] In *The Teacher Moves*, a book focusing on teacher nonverbal activity, Grant and Hennings describe episodes from videotapes of classroom teacher performance in which the teacher's physical clues contradicted the verbal stimuli she was emitting. In one instance recorded on tape, the teacher's recorded words suggested encouragement; students were being encouraged to ask questions. The stance, facial expression, and gestures of the teacher, however, said just the opposite. Interestingly enough, the students responded to the nonverbal component of the double-bind communication,

11. Kenneth Strongman as reported in the *Paterson News* by Robert Musel, August 5, 1970, p. 57.
12. Bryant and Wallace, *op. cit.*, p. 145.
13. Edward E. Sampson, *Social Psychology and Contemporary Society* (New York: Wiley, 1971), p. 61.

perhaps sensing that the physical stimuli carried the teacher's meaning more accurately than her words.[14]

Grant and Hennings further suggest that overuse of gesture and motion can be just as much a deterrent to communication as underuse. When a listener receives a steady barrage of motion and gesture, again there are no peaks. The listener has little to indicate what the speaker deems important, for the speaker's constant motion provides few clues and can even overstimulate the listener.[15] Delivery in this case is hyperintensive.

In discussing the communication media of our technological age, Marshall McLuhan writes: "In a culture like ours, long accustomed to splitting and dividing all things as a means of control, it is sometimes a bit of a shock to be reminded that, in operational and practical fact, the medium is the message."[16] In a face-to-face encounter, the body and voice are the media; in that respect, they are an integral part of the message.

Encounters with Voice and Body

1. Analyze your own vocal and physical language. Ask yourself:

    a. Is my speaking voice monotonous?

    b. Do I use gestures to speak for me?

    c. Am I physically overactive in communicating? underactive?

    d. What messages do I send through my facial expressions? Do my facial expressions add to or distract from my message?

    e. Are my words, body, and voice sending the same message, or do I send conflicting messages?

2. Using the same questions, listen to the way others around you use body and vocal language.

3. Begin to work on pitch variations in your voice. An activity devised by Harriet Grim may be helpful:[17]

    a. Speaking the sounds lightly, pronounce the syllable *la*, first taking it up the scale and then down. Keep each syllable distinct.

---

14. Barbara Grant and Dorothy Hennings, *The Teacher Moves* (New York: Teachers College Press, 1971), pp. 74, 76.
15. *Ibid.*, pp. 78, 80.
16. Marshall McLuhan, *Understanding Media* (New York: McGraw-Hill, 1964), p. 7.
17. Grim, *op. cit.*, p. 37.

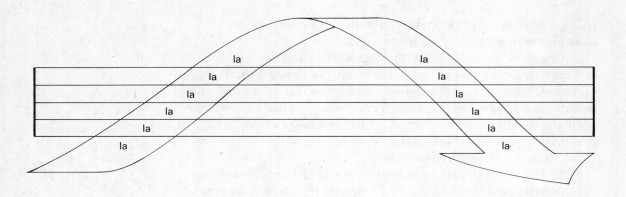

b. Substitute other syllables for *la*.

c. Reverse the direction of the tune and use words:

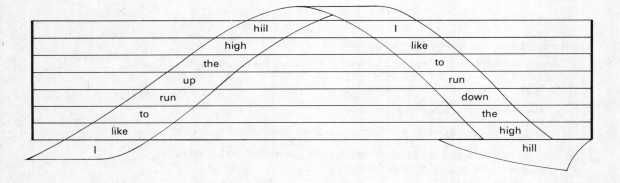

4. Begin to loosen up your inhibitions about physical expression. Listen to a recording of melodious, rhythmic music and "believe" you are swimming, you are swinging, you are golfing, you are painting a wall with big strokes, you are chopping wood. Physically interpret that activity to the music using all of your body. As Charles McGaw proposes, you must not *pretend;* you must believe you are![18]

5. To begin to become physically relaxed with expressive body motion, *believe* you are a jellyfish floating on the tide, a tree tossing in the wind, a horse trotting through the woods, Humpty Dumpty falling off the wall. Again, in the privacy of your room

---

18. Charles McGaw, *Acting Is Believing,* 2nd ed. (New York: Holt, Rinehart and Winston, 1966), p. 31.

to the accompaniment of a recorded musical selection, learn
what your body can express; become the jellyfish, the tree, the
horse, and so forth. As you express motion with your body,
relax and enjoy the sensation; as McGaw simply puts it, take it
easy.[19]

6. Working with other teachers or teachers-in-training, improvise
a dramatization of a story you all know, each taking a part in the
story, making your voice sound like that character's, and expressing physically the feelings and cognitive meanings of the story.
Good stories to use for this purpose are fairy tales because the
story line is generally known to group members; try "The
Three Little Pigs," "The Three Billy Goats Gruff," "The Emperor's
New Clothes," "Little Red Riding Hood," and "The Three Bears."

7. Pantomine can be used to tell a story. A narrator reads a story
as players nonverbally express story actions and feelings. Try this,
working with other teachers to loosen up your inhibitions about
using expressive body motion.

8. Working in study groups, select nursery rhymes to be told with
nonverbal language; observers can attempt to guess the rhyme
being "told."

9. Read a story to a group of children. Try to express the emotions
of the story vocally and facially. As you do this, keep your body
relaxed so that you can use it to supplement your voice when
the story action calls for physical expression. Repeat this activity several times with different stories.

10. Play with your voice. Take a selection from a magazine (advertisements work well). Read the selection a number of times,
each time expressing a different feeling toward the material.
Read as if you

are bored
are exasperated
think this is the greatest!
are unhappy
are in a hurry
are confiding in someone

Do the same with the telephone directory. Read down a column
expressing a particular emotion. Listeners can try to interpret
the emotion expressed.

---

19. *Ibid.*, p. 27.

WORD CONTROL

To say that voice and body have significant communication impact does not negate the fact that words are a major vehicle for transmitting cognitive and emotional meanings. In the first place, a speaker's choice of words gives some indication of his feelings toward a topic or person. What feeling do we communicate when we call a man *forthright*? In contrast, what feeling do we communicate when we call him *blunt*? Both words mean "outspoken"; however, the one has a positive connotation, the other negative.

The positive or negative connotation carried by words is a fundamental element of communication. Take four nouns that are considered synonyms: *ration*, *allowance*, *dole*, and *pittance*. Each means "an allotment of food, supplies, or money"; yet to refer to an allotment as a "ration" or "allowance" implies nothing negative. On the other hand, to call the same allotment a "dole" or "pittance" conveys a negative implication about the amount or the manner of distribution.

Sometimes too, use of a word in a context different from that in which it is commonly employed carries a negative connotation. For instance, the word *youngster* is a referent to elementary school children; in that context it has little emotional meaning. When a television reporter at a national convention refers to college-age demonstrators as "youngsters," however, he is expressing his own negative evaluation of the demonstrators. Similarly, taking a commonly known phrase or expression and putting it into a different context can imply some of the substance of the original expression. Remember Will Rogers' words: "I never met a man I didn't like." In the context: "Will Rogers never met Mr. X," the derived statement has a sarcastic ring.

Certain sentence patterns have communication value as well; consider, for example, "Do we want _____ or do we want_____?" The speaker employing that pattern inserts a personal belief as the first option and then proceeds to set up a straw horse as a second option: "Do we want to work together for peace or do we want the world to end in one nuclear blast?" Very often the speaker is actually implying that an opponent on the issue supports the undesirable option.

That certain words, phrases, and sentences can carry implied meaning is a major concern of a speaker. The speaker can take advantage of implied meanings to add impact and can become more aware of meanings sent unintentionally by implication. He needs to ask: "Am I communicating a negative feeling—which I really do not have—with words I have selected inappropriately or that carry hidden meanings? Do my words imply more than I intend? Can my words be construed differently than what I intend?"

These questions are essentially questions about the clarity of a verbal communication. A related problem can occur when a speaker who knows a subject well fails to realize that listeners may be functioning at a lower level of understanding. He takes for granted that listeners know the basic vocabulary, fails to include necessary background information, and selects examples too complex for beginners. Words, after all, are not just vehicles for sharing feelings but more fundamentally are vehicles for sharing complex thoughts. Especially when handling complex ideas, the speaker must ask: "Is the cognitive level of my message appropriate for the intended audience?"

Analyzing verbal control, a speaker can ask a range of questions about elements of verbal style. He can consider the following:

> *Complexity of sentence patterns*—Am I using complex and compound structures? Am I relying primarily on the simple sentence?
>
> *Variety of sentence patterns*—Am I drawing on imperative sentences, declarative patterns, rhetorical questions, complex and compound sentences? Am I repeating a single pattern?
>
> *Vocabulary level*—Am I using infrequently encountered words? Am I turning to words more commonly encountered?
>
> *Vocabulary scope*—Do I draw upon a large vocabulary? Do I restrict myself to a limited number of words?
>
> *Wordiness*—Am I using numbers of unnecessary words and sentences? Am I succinct? Am I overly brief?
>
> *Usage*—Am I using formal English, esoteric forms, standard English, a nonstandard dialect?
>
> *Personalism*—Am I employing terms that allow me to work informally with my listeners? Is my style more impersonal or formal?

A speaker can view each of these elements as a continuum along which a component of verbal style can be plotted:

Use of   Use of
Familiar Words   Uncommon Words

Nevertheless, a speaker would find it impossible to develop one map showing how he functions verbally in all social situations. Control of words implies control of vocabulary, usage, and sentence patterns to the extent that these elements can be varied as the audience varies. Obviously, we do not use the same patterns when talking to someone who has only recently learned English as we do with a person who speaks English fluently; with the first person we modify our verbal style, turning to simpler structures to carry the message. Obviously too, we speak more informally with friends than we do when we are seeking employment. The distinctiveness of such situations as these hits us so forcefully that we adjust our verbal style. In less distinctive situations, we may fail to adjust.

This is particularly true of new teachers fresh from academia. Entering a classroom for the first time as teachers, they may affect the sophisticated vocabulary and language patterns used in verbal exchanges with professors, and find that they are not communicating. First, the vocabulary may be beyond the comprehension of the students; second, the students may see the teacher as "not with it" and tune out.

Failure to adjust verbal language patterns to the situation sometimes results from rating one spot on any of the verbal continua as innately superior and adopting that style on all occasions. Using many different words rather than drawing upon a more limited vocabulary is not necessarily the way to communicate effectively; neither is speaking standard English inherently better than speaking a less common dialect. The preferred way of handling words is the mode that fits the situation. The pertinent question is, "Am I using words so that listeners understand and accept my message?" This is again a question of clarity.

A fourth question deals with impact: "Do I use the 'Language of Affective Communication' to heighten impact?" To S. I. Hayakawa, the language of affective communication is the language of alliteration, of metaphor and simile, of allusion, of repetitive patterns, of catchy titles and slogans. It is verbal language that tells us "what life feels like in the living."[20]

Affective devices have their place in both written and oral communication. Directing himself to the way the writer employs literary devices, Hayakawa in *Language in Thought and Action* discusses the literary use of *you* and *we* as an example of the way verbal communication can be styled to serve a purpose:

20. S. I. Hayakawa, *Language in Thought and Action*, 2nd ed. (New York : Harcourt Brace Jovanovich, 1939), p. 118.

[An] affective device is the *direct address* to the listener or reader, as "Keep off the grass. This means YOU!" . . . It softens the impersonality of formal speeches so that when a speaker or writer feels a special urgency about his message, he can hardly help using it. It occurs, therefore, in the finest rhetoric as well as in the simplest. An interesting variant of the "you" device occurs in the college classroom, when the learned professor says, "You will recall what Kropotkin says in his *Mutual Aid: A Factor in Evolution* . . ." although he knows very well that Mr. Merkle, sprawling in his chair at the back of the class, has never even heard of Kropotkin before.

Almost as common as the "you" device is the "we" device. . . . This device is particularly common in the politer forms of exhortation used by preachers and teachers. . . . The "we" device is also often heard in kindergarten and the lower elementary grades, where teachers use it to sugar-coat their disciplinary directives: "Now, Ricky, now, Penny, we don't fight and call each other names here. We'll all say we're sorry and sit down and be friends again, *won't we?*"[21]

Hayakawa further suggests that such devices as the metaphor, the simile, and personification are among "the most useful communicative devices we have, because by their quick affective power they often make unnecessary the inventing of new words." However, Hayakawa interjects a caution regarding overuse of devices such as the metaphor. Some metaphors have been so overworked that they have become "linguistic deadwood."

Encounters with Verbal Language

1. Tape twenty minutes of classroom interaction in which you play a major verbal role. Listen to the tape in playback several times using the questions on page 25 as an analysis guide. Do this on several occasions. Then draw some conclusions about the kinds of sentence patterns you tend to use, the level of vocabulary, your ability to be precise, and the like.

2. Study the tape, and make a chart on which you record your use of similes, metaphors, catchy slogans, allusions, and repetitive patterns. Again in retrospect consider what you were trying to achieve through the usage and whether the results were what you anticipated.

3. Restudy the tape, jotting down instances of your use of *you* and *we* as described by Hayakawa. In retrospect think about the purpose you were trying to achieve through this usage.

---

21. From *Language in Thought and Action*, Second Edition by S. I. Hayakawa, copyright, 1941, 1949, © 1963, 1964 by Harcourt Brace Jovanovich, Inc. and reprinted with their permission and the permission of George Allen & Unwin Ltd.

Examples of Use of *You* and *We*	Purposes for Which You Used This Style

4. Roleplay. Describe, chastise, explain, or relate using words that suggest you are matter-of-fact, slightly unhappy, or very upset. Then select a topic and explain it to a six-year-old, a teenager, a peer, your superior, a person who is just learning English.

5. Study several tapes of your classroom verbal interaction. Look for instances in which you used language to achieve a humorous effect. Record the instances on a chart you devise and evaluate the success or failure of the humor.

6. As you interact verbally in other settings, think about the verbal style you employ. Is it the same as in the classroom or do you adopt different verbal styles depending on where you are?

7. To get a notion of the positive and negative connotations carried by some words, try your hand at a task devised by Hayakawa in which you describe one phenomenon from different points of view depending on how close the phenomenon is to you.[22] For instance, the following sentence groups describe the same phenomenon—but from a different perspective:

   I am pleasingly plump. You are on the stout side. He is a mountain of jelly.

   I am friendly. You try to get along. She is on the pushy side.

   Write two sentences to go along with each of the following:

   a. I like to know what's going on. You _____ .
       He _____ .
   b. I always tell the truth. You _____ . She _____ .
   c. I _____ . You _____ . He is just plain stubborn.
   d. I _____ . You _____ . He demands perfection in everyone around him.
   e. I _____ . You _____ . She is a sloppy mess.

SITUATIONAL CONTROL

Messages are sent through manipulation of color, time, materials, living things, lighting, technological devices. These elements may be intentionally designed into a situation to send a specific message; in addition, situational elements may have been unintentionally built into the situation, and the speaker may be totally unaware of the messages they are carrying. This lack of awareness may be a block to communication if situational features are transmitting a message in conflict with the intended message.

The telecast of Richard Nixon's "Checkers Speech" of the 1952 election campaign is an instance in which careful control of situational variables paid off. The Republican vice-presidential nominee of that year was under heavy pressure to resign from his spot on the ticket as a result of disclosures about a secret campaign fund; the furor may not have equaled the furor raised by the Eagleton disclosures during the 1972 elections but the resulting pressure was, nonetheless, intense. Nixon met the pressure by taking his case before the nation in a telecast that was the epitome of high situational control. Using his family and their dog, Checkers, as props, he cast himself into the role of the honest, concerned,

---

22. Hayakawa, *op. cit.*, pp. 95-96.

family man. That he wielded situational variables to his advantage is indicated by the fact that he kept his place on the ticket. Recent political telecasts show a similar attempt to control situational variables.

Political figures are generally more adept at controlling situational variables than are teachers. As a candidate for president, Adlai Stevenson took political advantage of a picture showing a hole in the sole of his shoe; that picture of Stevenson was printed again and again to communicate that although Stevenson was wealthy, he was still an ordinary person. John Kennedy's references to Camelot, Lyndon Johnson's use of a rocking chair in a telecast with Walter Cronkite, and even Harry Truman and his piano were ways of taking advantage of the feelings people associate with objects and places.

When situational messages are ignored, the outcome can be disastrous. Remember the furor created among dog lovers over a news photo that showed Lyndon Johnson lifting up his favorite dog by its ears. In innocent disregard of public relations consequences, Johnson was simply enjoying playing with his dog. But dog lovers perceived him as being viciously cruel to the animal.

In everyday life, failure to wield situational variables efficiently can have similar repercussions. Consider one variable—furniture. Furniture—its kind and arrangement—does speak. A dean at one university had arranged his office so that his desk stood in the middle of the floor and visitors were seated 7 to 8 feet away from him across the desk. The chairs for visitors were leather office chairs, upright and with arms. With a reorganization within the administrative hierarchy, a new dean was assigned to that office space and made an immediate rearrangement of the furniture. He moved his desk closer to the wall, retaining the chairs-facing-the-desk arrangement. But in the area made vacant by the shift, he placed several comfortable chairs in a catercorner arrangement. There he conferred with professors rather than from behind his desk as his predecessor had done. Faculty members at the institution were quick to sense the significance of the change. The first dean was using space to say: "I am the dean. You are professors who must come to me"; the new dean was saying: "We are fellow workers who are discussing a common problem together." Only in infrequent instances did the second dean conduct a behind-the-desk interview; these were confrontation situations in which he purposefully used the design to send a different message.

Knowledge of situational variables is vital if we are to use design purposefully. Consider an example based on research. Studies indicate that "color does seem influential in generating movement," and "that greens and blues tend to generate less pronounced responses than reds."[23] Knowing this, we use red when we want to encourage high activity level, less vibrant colors when we want to communicate a sense of leisureliness. The designer of an environment can use this knowledge of color-activity relationships to send the desired message.

Amazingly—when we consider how important situational control is in social situations—we do very little in schools to help children understand and manipulate situational variables. Our perennial stress in language programs has been on verbal communication. Perhaps as we consider communication in classrooms, we need to keep in mind that mastery of the intricacies of communication is not just a necessity for the teacher but also for students whose work in classrooms is a laboratory experience in which they are learning skills so essential if their communication is to be effective.[24]

Encounters with Situational Messages

1. Analyze the way a "host" has manipulated situational elements. Consider:

   a. what his dress "says" about how he conceives of himself and of the situation
   b. what his design of furniture says
   c. whether he is intentionally using distance-control as part of his message
   d. whether he is intentionally using lighting-control and color-control as part of his message
   e. whether he is using time-control purposefully to get a message across

   The host can be your principal as he leads a faculty meeting or speaks with you in his office. He can be a professor with whom you are taking a college course, someone in whose home you are a guest, or the leader of a club activity.

---

23. Clifford Drew, "Psychological Behavioral Effects of the Physical Environment," *Review of Educational Research*, vol. 41, no. 5, December 1971, p. 457.

24. See *Smiles, Nods, and Pauses* by Dorothy G. Hennings (New York: Citation Press, 1974) for activities to develop children's nonverbal language skills.

2. In a situation, focus on just one variable such as furniture. Consider:

a. The Arrangement of Furniture—	Has the furniture been clustered into little groupings that encourage intimate conversation? Has it been lined up in a more formal arrangement in rows or around the edges of the room? Has the furniture arrangement allowed for some degree of individual activity?
b. The Kind of Furniture—	Is the furniture form-fitting and soft? hard and straight?
c. The Allotment of Seats—	Who gets or takes the best seat? Who is assigned to or selects the front row? What people sit together?

3. As you watch the nightly television news, watch for clues that indicate that politicians are using situational variables such as length of hair, manner of dress, objects such as cars, animals, members of their family intentionally to convey an impression. Do the same with stars being interviewed on television talk programs.

4. Think about your own self and the impression you convey situationally. Consider:

What does my hair style say about me?
What does the type of clothing I tend to select say about me?
What impression is created by the kind of people with whom I tend to associate?
What impression do I create through objects associated with me: my car, my house, my glasses, etc.?

MODULE 3
Encountering Barriers to Communication

MODULE GOALS

The teacher gains competency in—

recognizing masking behavior

identifying the components of the filter through which he views communication

recognizing differences in the way people perceive a message

hypothesizing reasons for wandering behavior

identifying wandering behavior indicated nonverbally

Often a conversationalist or a speaker leaves an encounter feeling that he has sent a clear message and has understood what the other has said. This is probably not true. Communication is fraught with stumbling blocks; misunderstanding of the message and inability to transmit ideas exactly as intended are common. At least three elements can block communication—*masking*, *filtering*, and *wandering*.

MASKING

Erving Goffman in *The Presentation of Self in Everyday Life* proposes that often in human encounters participants maintain an outward front or facade that does not necessarily reflect their inner feelings or thoughts. This facade is projected to present the self in a favorable light, to conform to established patterns of behavior associated with a specific situation or role, to create a special effect, and/or to control the behavior of others functioning in the situation. Goffman cites as an example the "adoption of a social face" as it occurs on Shetland Isle. Neighbors, dropping in for the traditional cup of tea, can be observed making an abrupt change in facial expression just before reaching the door of the home visited; at the point at which they come under observation, they assume the outward markings typically associated with calling on a neighbor.[1]

In an article in the October 1971 issue of *Theory into Practice*, Charles Galloway applies Goffman's term *impression management* to youngsters' attempts to manipulate their own behavior to create

---

1. Erving Goffman, *The Presentation of Self in Everyday Life* (Garden City, N.Y.: Doubleday Anchor Books, 1959), p. 8.

an effect and suggests that students soon acquire the facial expressions and gestures expected of them in school. As Galloway states, students "can be seen to look as if they are listening, to appear busy with their assignments, and to nod their heads to show they understand the teacher's explication and instructions."[2]

That this is so can be verified simply by recalling our own performances in social situations. We have all feigned attention at some point; faced with a boring companion, we may have painted a smile on our faces, nodded our heads vigorously, and leaned forward focusing on him while our thoughts were millions of miles away. What we were doing was using learned gestures and facial expressions to create the impression of attention.

Situational clues—time, space, attire, setting—can be used in much the same way. For example, teachers may dress for the role of teacher; they wear only those garments that conform to their image of what a teacher is and reject garments that do not conform. Likewise, youths who turn to blue jeans, tee-shirts, and bare feet are building an image that says something about their sense of freedom and their disdain of materialism. They too are involved in impression management.

Words can be used to mask genuine feelings and thoughts. Have you ever said, "Yes, I'd love to go," because it was expected of you? In truth, you had a headache and would have preferred to stay home. Such half-truths are used to help another participant maintain the facade he is projecting, to gain acceptance by the group, or to ease a possibly offensive situation. In such cases, the speaker is deliberately creating an illusion.

How does the listener see through a masking of true feelings? According to Goffman, there are elements within a masking situation that conflict. A message sent verbally may be contradicted by messages transmitted physically and situationally. Goffman uses the example of how one cook determines the success of her culinary efforts. Instead of taking the consumer's message at face value, she watches the way in which he raises fork to mouth, the way in which he puts the food into his mouth, and even the manner in which he chews it.[3]

In essence, what the perceptive listener does is to focus on

2. Charles Galloway, "The Challenge of Nonverbal Research," *Theory into Practice*, vol. 10, no. 4, October 1971, p. 312.
3. Goffman, *op. cit.*, p. 7.

the subtle elements of the communication. It is easy to string
together words that mask what one really feels and to deliver those
words with a false enthusiasm. It is more difficult to paint an expression of eagerness, sadness, or hurt on one's face and to affect
a particular gesture pattern. But to control the tension of the
muscles, the rising color of face and neck, heavy swallowing and
breathing, wrinkles on brow and next to eyes, nervous shaking of
hands and knees is almost impossible. As Ewan Grant notes after
more than seven years of studying how people communicate word-
lessly: "While it is easy enough to lie with words, it is extremely
difficult to disguise true emotions coming through in nonverbal
signals."[4]

How can a listener become sensitive to tell-tale, nonverbal
signals? One approach is to observe a person as he interacts with
people with whom he feels secure. Interacting with close friends
and family members, he may "let down his hair." His mask of
words and action may slip away, and his communication may more
accurately reflect his genuine feelings. Now when the listener observes the person in more threatening situations, he may be able to
perceive subtle differences which indicate that some part of the performance is a mask. The observer's knowledge of a person's un-
threatened communication pattern provides a framework for judging
the validity of a particular unit of communication.

Of course, having observed a person in a number of different
social situations makes it still more possible for the listener to develop
a framework for judging. From a first encounter with the hypothetical Mr. Chisholm introduced in Module 1, one can depart with a
picture of a stiff man with a big ego. His posting of diplomas, his
offering the visitor a hard chair, his selecting that large desk, his
keeping the prospective employee waiting convey this impression.
But as one gets to know Chisholm, one sees that he is a scholarly,
rather shy man who enjoys books more than people and feels
insecure about how people view him. For him the diplomas, chairs,
desk, even his meticulous dress are ways of bolstering his own
confidence in himself and make interaction easier for him; they
are part of his facade.

Whether or not a participant is right in masking true feelings
is an obvious next question. Clearly, in some situations one has a
responsibility to carry on even when feeling less than happy or even

---

4. Ewan Grant as reported in the *Paterson News*, Aug. 5, 1970.

physically unwell. A teacher with a headache still tries to communicate interest despite the fact that at that moment he must feign enthusiasm. Or coming to school angry after an exchange with his wife, a man tries not to let that anger show; containing his feelings, he presents a serene countenance to students. Or responsible for children during an emergency, the teacher masks his own fright behind a calm exterior to prevent the children from panicking.

A judgment about the rightness of masking the true self in more complex situations is more difficult to make. Where do we draw the line between an unconscionable hypocrisy and a social amenity? Each individual must judge for himself. This book attempts only to describe an element that does exist in human communication and can become a barrier to accurate transmission of thoughts and feelings.

Encounters with Masking

1. As you listen to others converse, watch for subtle clues that indicate the speaker is masking true feeling. Watch for

   a. a slight hesitation that indicates a speaker is less than enthusiastic about doing something
   b. signs of irritation, anger, fear, unhappiness masked behind a calm exterior—shaking hands, blushing, tightening of the lips, heavy swallowing
   c. gestures and facial expressions that contradict the spoken message
   d. tensions of the muscles that conflict with a calm tone of voice
   e. an abrupt change—an initial reaction covered up immediately

2. If you have the opportunity to observe in a classroom, look for verbal and nonverbal clues that indicate that students are employing masking behavior. Do the same with the teacher.
3. If you are working with a group of children in a classroom, observe their behavior patterns in the classroom, in the playground, in the lunch room. Try to identify clues that suggest when a child is really attentive and really interested—not just pretending.

FILTERING

Stage an emotion-ladened incident such as an argument or an accident before a group of teachers or teacher-interns. Immediately afterward, all witnesses write a description of what happened. What will result is a slightly different interpretation by each observer.

That individuals perceive identical stimuli differently is supported by the extensive experimental studies by F. C. Bartlett. In Bartlett's experiments, research subjects viewed for brief intervals simple and complex designs, concrete representations, and complex pictures. After viewing the materials, subjects either drew what they saw (as in the case of simple designs) or told what they saw (as in the case of complex pictures).

Bartlett reports that especially in tests with complex picture materials an "extraordinary variety of interpretation" was produced by observers of an identical stimulus. For example, having viewed the painting "Hubert and Arthur" by Yeames, one subject described the painting as a little girl praying at her mother's knee. A second saw two people wrestling; a third saw a representation of Othello and Desdemona; and a fourth saw Charles the First and Henrietta.[5] Amazingly, all had viewed the same stimulus!

From his studies Bartlett concludes that much of what a person perceives is an inference and that the interests and attitudes of a person are determinants of what he perceives in a situation. One specific determinant is self-concern. Personal insecurity, for instance, can lead a person to interpret a message as a threat to self when no negative message is being sent. Consider the ego-tied interpretations in the following situations:

> A superior fails to greet you as you pass. Your ego-based interpretation—He is mad at me. Possible explanation—He is so engrossed in a problem he simply fails to see you.
>
> A junior high girl passes a note to another girl. Your ego-based interpretation as the teacher—She is trying to defy me. Possible explanation—The girl just broke up with her boyfriend; she must confide in her girlfriend.

Likewise, what a person values, likes, dislikes, judges as right can determine how he or she receives a message. A speaker's use of distance, eye focus, gesture, situational elements, tone and loudness of voice, words, sentence patterns can be perceived positively by one listener, negatively by another—dependent on the listeners' personal preferences.

The meaning attached to words by different people is another determinant. A child of kindergarten age is told that a doctor will be visiting his classroom. When the visitor arrives, the child approaches

---

5. F. C. Bartlett, *Remembering: A Study in Experimental and Social Psychology* (Cambridge, England: Cambridge University Press, 1967), pp. 17-33.

with: "I don't like you. You stick needles in people." The visitor—a college professor and doctor of education—is confused until she realizes that the child is functioning on a limited concept of *doctor*. Told that a doctor is to visit, the child who has previously encountered only medical doctors assumes that an M.D. is coming; the child views what the teacher says with distaste, waiting unhappily for the doctor and the needles to arrive.

Such a misunderstanding between a child cognitively functioning at what Jean Piaget has identified as the preoperational stage and an adult could be predicted from the emerging research on language development. An example will clarify just one difference between the child's and the adult's view of a word. Working with double-function words (for example, such words as *sweet*, *hard*, *cold*, *crooked*, which can refer to physical objects and to psychological feelings about people), Asch and Nerlove found that children between three and six years old tend to apply double-function words to physical objects; only in a few cases, do children apply the words to a person. Using double-function words to apply to both physical and psychological phenomena is more common after age seven, although children still have difficulty at this age talking about the meanings attached to the words in both contexts. By age twelve, youngsters show "a noticeable advance in the comprehension of the dual function."[6]

Dialectal differences can pose a similar barrier between participants in an interaction. A dialect is any one of the mutually comprehensible regional and social varieties of a natural language. Varieties of a language differ in the meanings attached to words, pronunciation, sentence patterns, and spelling conventions.

On a motoring trip through England, you would quickly discover the barriers to communication posed by dialectal differences. A car in front of you might bear the sign "Running in. Please pass." A speaker of the local dialect would know that the car is a new one being driven slowly; it would take you longer to get the message. In America we *break in* not *run in*. Experienced travelers, of course, know that they face a different language situation and consequently, they adjust their listening. Then, too, travelers generally do not make value judgments; they do not consider their own dialect superior to what they would encounter in England.

---

6. Solomon Asch and Harriet Nerlove, "The Development of Double Function Terms in Children: An Exploratory Investigation," in Bernard Kaplan and Seymour Wapner (eds.), *Perspectives in Psychological Theory: Essays in Honor of Heinz Werner* (New York: International Universities Press, 1960), pp. 47-60.

Encountering dialectal differences within the United States, however, speakers of standard American English may fail to adjust listening habits and may make value judgments. Speakers of some dialects of American English—Black, Cajun, Appalachian, Pidgeon— have been made to feel that theirs is an inferior way of speaking. Even a teacher may pose this barrier to communication. Rather than encouraging young children to express themselves in their dialect, the teacher may not listen to what the child is saying; he "corrects" and implies that the speaker is stupid, lazy, or wrong. In actuality, it is the teacher who has failed to understand the nature of dialects. Not realizing that in a diverse country "there exists an almost infinite series of local dialects,"[7] the teacher throws roadblocks in the path of communication based on his own perception of what is verbally right.

Even as words do not mean the same to everyone so nonverbal expressions mean different things to different people. Anthropologists who have investigated the ways various cultural groups express themselves suggest that cultural groups associate different meanings with a specific action. For instance, in *The Hidden Dimension*, Edward T. Hall—the anthropologist who has studied in detail the meaning of distance in human interaction—provides examples of how different national groups interpret an act. Whereas Americans tend to interpret hushed voices as a brewing conspiracy, the English modulate their voices "for to be overheard is to intrude on others." French men do not hestiate to visually analyze women they pass on the streets; American women unaccustomed to a thorough looking-over from American men read more into the French men's act than the senders intend. Arabs "consistently breathe on people when they talk"; to deny others "your breath is to act ashamed." In contrast, Americans are uncomfortable conversing at breath-range; they feel that being breathed upon is an infringement of their personal territory.[8]

Ashley Montagu, in *Touching: The Human Significance of the Skin*, makes a similar point about direct physical contact in diverse cultures. He suggests that tactile communication is far more common among the Russians, Jews, and speakers of languages having Latin roots than among the English or the Germans. For instance, physical expression of affection between father and son typically does not

7. Joseph Friend, *An Introduction to English Linguistics* (New York: World Publishing, 1967), p. 92.
8. Edward T. Hall, *The Hidden Dimension* (Garden City, N.Y.: Doubleday and Company, 1966), pp. 134, 135, 149.

occur in England and Germany after a boy has grown up. Contrast this with the way in which French men embrace and kiss their male friends and Arab men join hands with men with whom they are walking. Such a show of affection embarrasses the American, who, according to Montagu, tends to be less tactually oriented than the French but more tactual than either the British or Germans.[9]

Obviously when cultures meet, misinterpretation of nonverbal messages can occur. In addition, if we remember that Americans have diverse ethnic backgrounds, we can hypothesize that such misunderstanding is probable within the geographical United States. Even among Americans there are differences in the way groups of people interpret not only distance and physical contact but also gestures, facial expressions, and posture or stance. These differences can become barriers to communication.

Encounters with Filtering

1. As you listen to people sending messages to you, analyze your own reactions. Map the personal filter through which you sift impressions.

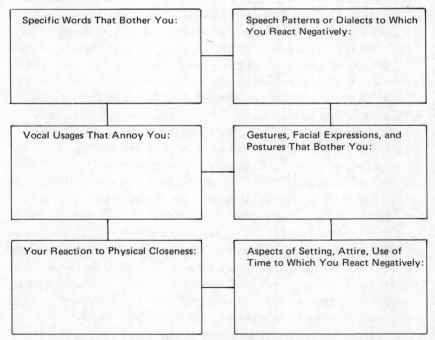

Specific Words That Bother You:	Speech Patterns or Dialects to Which You React Negatively:
Vocal Usages That Annoy You:	Gestures, Facial Expressions, and Postures That Bother You:
Your Reaction to Physical Closeness:	Aspects of Setting, Attire, Use of Time to Which You React Negatively:

9. Ashley Montagu, *Touching: The Human Significance of the Skin* (New York: Columbia University Press, 1971), pp. 260-272.

2. Study your own reaction to messages in terms of the following questions. Look for specific examples in your own behavior to support your analysis.

> Do I make ego-based interpretations? very often? often? sometimes?
>
> Do I "get my back up" early in a conversation and use my irritation as a filter for the rest of the interaction? very often? often? sometimes?
>
> Do I consider the dialect I speak as the correct one? Do I look down on those who speak differently? generally? sometimes? never?
>
> Am I embarrassed by affection shown to me by others? generally? sometimes? never?
>
> Am I impatient with children who have a more limited concept of words than adults have? generally? sometimes? never?

3. Replicate the Bartlett experiment described in this section. Make a collection of simple and complex designs by drawing designs on large pieces of white cardboard. Locate concrete pictures such as those in the *Many Faces of Youth* series distributed by Developmental Learning Materials, Chicago, and abstract pictures such as those in the *Modern Art Series* distributed by F. A. Owen, Dansville, New York. Sequentially show four or five designs or pictures to a group of young people. Youngsters describe or draw what they see. Compare interpretations.

4. Replicate the Asch-Nerlove study with children of successive age groups. Give the children such words as *warm, crooked, hard, sweet* to use in sentences. Older children write their sentences; younger children individually tell their sentences into a tape recorder. Analyze the data to see how children of different ages conceive of the words. Do they use the words strictly in the physical sense? Do they apply the words to people using a more abstract meaning?

·5. Devise experiments to study the components of the filters that people use to view messages they are receiving. For example, you may want to work with the way people view different dialects or varying amounts of language sophistication. Play the tape to numbers of subjects who must rank the dialects as to the one they prefer first, the one preferred next, and so on. You can do the same thing with aspects of dress, setting, facial features, gestures, posture.

WANDERING

A participant enters a social situation accompanied by his own thoughts, problems, and concerns that may be far different from the topic under general discussion. These concerns interfere with the participant's ability to focus on what is being said. As a result, his attention jumps back and forth between the personal problem and the discussion topic.

Every teacher has probably found himself considering what activity he will organize next rather than focusing completely on a student who is speaking. A young boy who has come to school after having an argument with a parent may find his mind slipping from an interesting discussion to return to the unpleasantness just experienced. In these instances, an overriding concern precludes the listener's giving full attention to a message being sent and poses a communication barrier.

Wandering behavior can also take the form of anticipating. Anticipators are listeners who think they know what the speaker is going to say before he says it. Anticipators assume that having heard other people expound on the topic, they need not attend to what is being said; their thoughts turn elsewhere.

R. E. Myers in an article in the March 1971 issue of the *Grade Teacher* suggests that anticipatory listening is a common trait of teachers.[10] Teachers anticipate the end of a student's sentence before the student has finished expressing the thought and interrupt the student in mid-sentence. Additionally, according to Myers, teachers are guilty of focusing on grammatical constructions rather than really listening to the content of a student's message.

Another form of wandering is mental waiting; here listeners are cognitively involved in formulating their own ideas rather than concentrating on the speaker. These listeners are waiting for a momentary lull into which they can interject their thoughts. In a sense, these listeners put themselves in a holding position until they themselves have an opportunity to speak.

Listeners also let their minds go completely blank and become nonreceivers. Perhaps mental exhaustion, the drone of voices, the hum of a motor, the monotony of a repetitive task, or the warmth of the room has lulled the listener into a sleeplike trance. Whatever the cause, he does not "hear" the message being sent.

---

10. R. E. Meyers, "Listening," *Grade Teacher*, vol. 81, no. 7, March 1971, pp. 30-31.

Listeners can indulge in limited reception. They can focus on the verbal stimuli and not attend to the physical, vocal, or situational stimuli. They can be preoccupied with elements in the situation and fail to perceive messages sent through words and actions. In classrooms today there is much stress on interpreting verbal messages; youngsters spend time learning new vocabulary, outline form, or sentence structure. In contrast, little stress is placed on interpreting messages sent nonverbally. How often do we ask children or youth to note the gestures a performer uses to show concern for others? How often do we ask children or youth to look at the dress of an entertainer and interpret the messages that attire is sending? How often do we ask children or youth to analyze the distances at which they are comfortable interacting? Rarely! As a result people grow up wearing "communication blinders" with little knowledge of how to listen to complete messages and the tendency to rely on verbal listening.

Encounters with Wandering

1. As you watch a listener, look for bodily signals that indicate his attention has wandered. Look for a change of eye focus, a glazed look of the eyes, a change in body tensions. When you perceive wandering behavior, hypothesize possible causes: preoccupation with other thoughts, fatigue, your own droning style, his anticipation of what you are saying.
2. If you are observing classroom interaction, look for clues that suggest that students' attention is wandering. Hypothesize reasons for their behavior.
3. Watch for anticipatory listening in your own classroom interaction. Do you cut a student off in mid-sentence? Do you correct a student's usage even as he is talking? Tape a segment of classroom discussion, and identify specific examples of anticipatory listening and interruption.
4. Wandering can affect a speaker as well as a listener. Speaking may lack the tight organization more characteristic of written prose. The speaker begins to talk about one subject, then shifts to another. Each thought triggers others until he has rambled far from his original point, and perhaps has lost his audience. Study a taped episode of your own classroom verbal behavior to see if your verbal style is typified by wandering.

5. When you leave a social situation, ask yourself whether some messages sent in the situation were interpreted differently from the way intended. Why did this happen? What barriers to communication were present? Give specific examples to verify your conclusions. In a classroom do an analysis of the specific communication barriers present during a particular time period.

A GUIDE TO ANALYZE CLASSROOM COMMUNICATION BARRIERS

Evidences of Masking		Evidences of Filtering		Evidences of Wandering	
Teacher	*Students*	*Teacher*	*Students*	*Teacher*	*Students*

THE TEACHER AS RECEIVER-DECODER

Very often teachers conceive their role in the classroom as speakers-tellers-directors-organizers, viewing students as receivers of teacher-encoded messages. Such a conception is limited and limiting. Based on a comprehensive model of communication, teaching must be redefined to include receiving-decoding as a pivotal component.

Because teaching has sometimes been equated with speaking, in developing our communication competencies, let us begin first by focusing on the receiving-decoding side of the teaching process. Module 4 supplies the teacher and the teacher-intern with guides for analyzing student nonverbal messages and helps the teacher develop competencies in receiving nonverbal feedback. Module 5 focuses on student verbal talk and helps the teacher gain competency in interpreting the cognitive operations represented by student statements, in interpreting implied meanings, and in accepting differences in verbal language. Again a category system is included as a guide for distinguishing different kinds of statements.

One caution about using the category systems: These systems are not intended as systematic instruments through which classroom interaction can be studied with a high degree of reliability; it is not intended that readers try to categorize precisely every verbal and nonverbal utterance observed. Rather the systems are guides through which teachers can become more aware of the kinds of utterances to look for and the significance of different kinds of nonverbal and verbal messages. Increased receptivity to student messages is the goal sought.

MODULE GOALS

The teacher gains competency in—

developing nonverbal profiles of students
perceiving changes in typical motion patterns of students
interpreting nonverbal feedback generated by students,
    especially behavior signaling restlessness
using nonverbal behavior to perceive facades students
    construct
judging the effectiveness of his own teaching by analyzing
    nonverbal feedback

MODULE 4
Listening for
Nonverbal Messages

Arlene Rickenbauch was working with her second grade class to
develop understanding of the way words are changed structurally
to reflect past action. She asked questions that encouraged children
to give sentences about something that happened yesterday. She
recorded the children's contributions on an experience chart, asking
them to underline "the words that let us know it happened yesterday." Most of the children were attentive; they raised their hands to
participate, focusing their eyes on teacher and chart. Several children,
as would be natural in any class, were slouching in their chairs; some
propped their heads on their arms while others watched and said
nothing.

Half-way through the lesson, Miss Rickenbauch stopped in mid-
sentence. She glanced at one boy who was slouching in his chair with
head propped on an up-raised arm and asked, "Jeff, are you OK?"
Jeff complained that he did not feel well and was hustled off to the
nurse. A short time later he returned to class to get his coat; he was
being sent home.

After the activity had ended, the teacher was asked how she
knew that something was wrong with Jeff. She explained that Jeff
was typically an active participant in discussions, waving his hand
back and forth to join in and keeping his body in constant motion.
But today Jeff was passive. The teacher's question was an answer to
Jeff's nonverbal message.

Children and youth in classrooms are constantly sending messages
with their bodies. Ability to perceive these messages, note changes in
typical motion patterns, interpret nonverbal feedback, and modify
one's actions in response are part of the stock-in-trade of a teacher.
To master classroom communication, the teacher must learn to
"listen" to the body language of students.

One form of physical language is students' *language of participation*. Some body talk is emitted as students contribute directly to class interaction and attend to the work; body motion is a vehicle through which students send messages as they encounter learning-oriented activities of the classroom either individually or in groups.

A second kind of body talk that students use—the *language of being*—has more to do with the child or youth as a person than with his role as a student participant in a learning situation. Students respond to internal and external stresses, allow their attention to wander, attempt to socialize or distract, and move to get themselves into a position so that they can do something else.

A third type of motion—*the language of heightening*—makes meanings more emphatic or explicit: body language is used to clarify or emphasize what is said verbally. Heightening motions communicate messages such as "This is important," or "It looks like this." These motions are observed wherever people encounter and converse with others—on street corners, over back fences, as well as within classrooms. These motions are integral elements within any system of communication.

Figure 4-1   Nonverbal Messages of Students

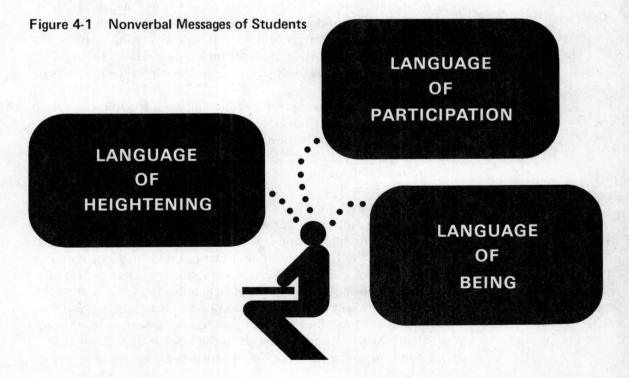

A classification system based on the language of participation, the language of being, and the language of heightening can serve as a guide for teachers as they informally observe and study the behavior of young people in classrooms. Module 4 presents such a system to the teacher who wants to become more receptive to students' nonverbal language.

THE LANGUAGE OF PARTICIPATION

The language of participation takes two forms. One form is a direct contribution to classroom activity; the other occurs when a student engages the things of learning as an individual and his participation makes no immediate contribution to other participants. The body language elicited in the first instance can be called *contributing*; in the second instance *engaging*.

Contributing Motions

Students participate in classroom learning in ways that place them in the center of the activity and involve them directly with others. For example, a student may contribute nonverbally to a discussion, demonstrate before the class, make a move in a game, speak nonverbally in a dramatic performance, help with classroom chores. In each of these instances, the student is participating actively with teacher and/or other students on learning-related matters: what he is doing adds to the learning and/or involvement of others.

Joining   One kind of nonverbal contribution is the *joining* motions of students. Students make numbers of motions that indicate a desire to join the interaction: waving the hand, leaning forward, moving abruptly, holding the arm high in the air, pointing. Less obvious joining motions more typical of secondary school participants are those in which only an eyebrow is raised, a slight smile occurs, or the eyes light up.

Joining motions occur as students form their own work groups in less structured classrooms. If a girl wants to work with a friend, she may tap the friend on the shoulder or move into a neighboring position. Joining is more covert when a student is less certain of a positive reception or is older. A glance, a fleeting smile, a tilt of the head may be the only signal that he wants to join a group. The same is true of motions made to gain teacher attention. Some are distinct; the participant walks up to the teacher or gestures with his hand. In contrast, some joining motions are nearly imperceptible.

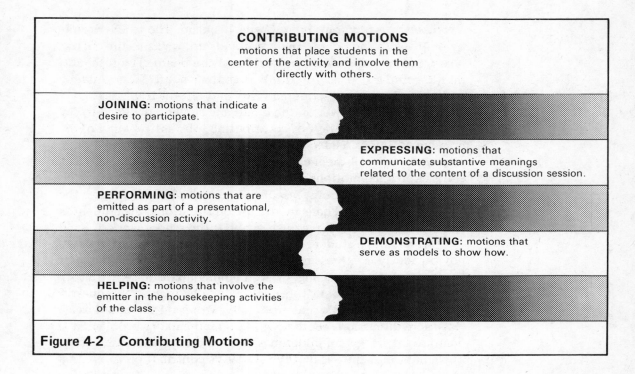

CONTRIBUTING MOTIONS
motions that place students in the
center of the activity and involve them
directly with others.

JOINING: motions that indicate a
desire to participate.

EXPRESSING: motions that
communicate substantive meanings
related to the content of a discussion session.

PERFORMING: motions that are
emitted as part of a presentational,
non-discussion activity.

DEMONSTRATING: motions that
serve as models to show how.

HELPING: motions that involve the
emitter in the housekeeping activities
of the class.

Figure 4-2   Contributing Motions

Students may also help in the selection of others who want to
contribute. A participant may make a motion to draw the teacher's
attention to another student whose raised hand had been unper-
ceived by the teacher; a student may assume the role of teacher
and call on participants.

One example from actual classroom interaction indicates the
importance of a teacher's perceiving joining motions. Fred had
made overt moves to join two other boys working on a word puzzle,
but the responding motions of the two boys made clear that Fred
had been told to "get lost." Fred went back to his own seat to
work by himself. His attention was momentary; he was up shortly
to go to the boys' room. When he returned, he announced, "I
quit. You're not going to get me to do this any more!" The teacher,
however, had seen the earlier rejecting motions directed at Fred.
Now she said nothing. Instead, she walked over to another group
working near Fred, began to help them, waved to Fred to move his
chair over, and nonverbally included him in her explanation. Without hesitation, Fred began to work with the group.

Expressing   A boy joins in by raising his hand. The teacher responds by pointing to the board. The boy stands up, walks to the chalkboard, picks up the chalk, and writes on the board. The teacher asks the student, "Can you think of another point?" The student shakes his head in a responding "No" and returns to his seat.

Writing the answer on the board and shaking the head to say "No" are nonverbal ways of contributing substantively and of expressing meanings related to the content of the lesson. For this reason, we can call them *expressing* motions. Most often the student emits expressing motions when he reacts negatively or positively, asks or answers questions, responds to a command, or focuses the attention of others. These are discussion situations; the student is communicating with someone else about the school work at hand.

When does a student specifically use expressing motions? A boy obviously is expressing nonverbally when he replies to a question by nodding, grimacing, or even pulling up his nose. He also expresses when he points to a spot on a globe to answer a question, moves his lips to read a sentence orally, writes on the board as a classroom discussion recorder, works a mathematics problem at the board as others watch, underlines an item on a chalkboard listing. The common feature is that the student's contribution is one that other participants are expected to focus on as part of the ongoing interaction.

Student participants use similar expressing motions when they work together in small groups. If young people are cooperating on a mathematics problem, a girl may work the example on paper as the others follow her motions with their eyes. At times too, young people may be involved in an interaction in which one youngster tutors others. In this case, the "teacher" may point to sentences that the others must read and may send correct-wrong signals with his body. The "learners" may simultaneously be responding through a variety of gestures, facial changes, and body movements as well as through verbal communication.

Performing   Another way in which students contribute to ongoing class activity is through motions produced as part of a group sports event, a physically oriented classroom game, a dramatic activity, or an exhibition. These are nondiscussion types of activities in which the give-and-take of ideas is not central. In some instances, there may be an audience watching the performing motions. A few examples will clarify. Students perform when they run the bases in a baseball game

    make dance steps as part of a class social dancing activity

    hop up and down as actors in a class performance of *H.M.S. Pinafore*

    gesture as part of the flag salute

    jiggle bells as part of a rhythm band activity

    play solos on musical instruments

    manipulate equipment as part of a science experiment that others are
        watching

In each instance, the students are adding to the activity in which others are involved.

Demonstrating   When students perform, they are not serving as models of how-to-do. In contrast, when they demonstrate, their motions are models of how to carry out a task; watchers are supposed to be studying details of the movement to find out how to do it. Students demonstrate when they

    move their feet in a dance step as others watch to see how it is done

    make swishing motions with a brush to show how to apply paint

    connect apparatus to show others how to connect theirs

Students in classrooms typically emit demonstrating motions when they are showing others, are presenting reports with an element of "how to do it," and are involved in physically oriented activities often found in science, art, sports, industrial arts. Students emitting demonstrating motions are assuming a definite leadership role.

Helping   A bell rings somewhere in the school. Noise of movement filters through an open door. A boy, sensing the interference, closes the door. His motion in this case involves him in the housekeeping chores of a classroom. In short, he is helping. Students emit helping motions when they

    wash beakers after a science experiment

    erase the board

    set up, run, and dismantle audiovisual equipment

    distribute paper

    adjust blinds

Activities for Analyzing Contributing Motions

1. Identify contributing motions made by students in a classroom in which you are observing or on a videotape you are watching. On the recording chart on page 54, list specific motions you observe that fall into each category.

EXAMPLES OF CONTRIBUTING MOTIONS				
Joining	*Expressing*	*Performing*	*Demonstrating*	*Helping*

2. Using a chart similar to that in activity 1, analyze a videotaped recording of student contributing motions elicited in response to your teaching. You may find few motions indicative of helping or demonstrating activity or you may find that expressing motions are directed by students to the teacher and rarely to other students. This may indicate that you tend to do the performing and are not allowing students to take initiative or leadership roles. Information of this type can help you make judgments about the effectiveness of your teaching.

3. Focus on the contributing moves of one student participant to determine the kinds of contributions that typify his performance. Questions to consider include: Does the participant tend to

    hide his contribution in unison-type activities?
    make his contribution primarily in a helping capacity?
    emit expressing motions primarily in large group discussions? in small
       group discussions? in one-to-one conversations?
    emit large numbers of joining in motions?
    emit relatively few performing or demonstrating motions?

4. As you gather information on a student's typical contributing motions, you may wish to compile your data on a profile chart similar to the one shown on page 56; list specific motions emitted that fall into each subcategory.

5. Draw conclusions about a student's typical contributing motions from the chart developed in activity 4. Attempt to identify the categories of motion that typify his classroom contribution.

6. Use the contribution profile you have constructed to sense genuine feelings hidden beneath a facade the student may construct. As noted in Module 1, the motions made by a participant can tell an observer as much as or more than his words. For example, a child may verbally respond with a "Yes, I'll do that"; yet his body may simultaneously be saying "No." See if you can identify specific instances of this phenomenon in your classroom.

7. As you study contributing motions emitted by students, look for the I-am-thoroughly-involved motions that students make so they will not have to become contributing participants. Often as a teacher receives joining signals from some participants, he receives I-am-thoroughly-involved signals from others;

CONTRIBUTING PROFILE OF _____

Joining Motions

Kinds of joining motions: Conditions under which they occur:
1.
2.
     etc.

TYPES OF MOTION PATTERNS STUDENT JOINS

Expressing
1. total class
2. small group
3. one-to-one
   with teacher
   with other students

Performing In
1. sports
2. dramatics
3. exhibitions
4. unison activities

Demonstrating
1. to teacher
2. to large groups
3. to small groups
4. to an individual

Helping
1. spontaneous motions
2. motions emitted on request

---

students look down at their books, begin to write intensely, assume a serious, pensive expression. These motions are intended to tell the teacher that the students are too busy to contribute; actually the students may be attempting to avoid contributing.

Engaging Motions

A student may be mentally active, highly involved, and aware without contributing directly to the total learning environment and without being the focus of others' attention. The student is simply engaged with the materials or ideas on an individual basis.

When students are interacting with the materials and ideas of learning, they can be observed emitting three types of engaging motions: (1) motions through which they maintain a focus on others contributing to the interaction or on materials related to the learning activity, (2) motions giving the appearance that students are seriously considering ideas or materials, (3) motions occurring as students pursue an activity on their own without interacting with or focusing on others.

Focusing   Motions emitted as students attend to classroom inter-action and materials can be termed *focusing* motions. Focusing motions are primarily associated with the participant's role as a listener, watcher, or waiter. Examples of focusing motions include:

> Leaning forward in chair to focus on speaker
> Moving head back and forth to follow the give-and-take of a discussion, the action on stage, the action of a sports event
> Orienting the body in the direction of a speaker
> Waiting at seat for class to begin

When participants emit focusing motions, they are looking on rather than doing themselves. Interestingly enough, most total class discussions stimulate a great deal of focusing behavior. In a discussion, only one can contribute at a time; others must look on or wait their opportunity to contribute.

Considering   Sometimes looking on can be more active than main-taining an orientation toward events occurring in the classroom. Students emit more overt signals that say they are mentally encoun-tering ideas and materials. They can be observed

> shaking their heads in disagreement with remarks made by a speaker
> smiling broadly at a joke cracked by a speaker
> clapping during a performance
> gesturing in excitement during a sports event
> pursing lips in thought

Such considering motions do not involve participants as active con-tributors; their nods, frowns, head-shakes are not *the* answers others in the class are focusing on. However, these motions do provide the teacher with feedback as to whether he is getting the message across.
Considering motions may involve students with instructional

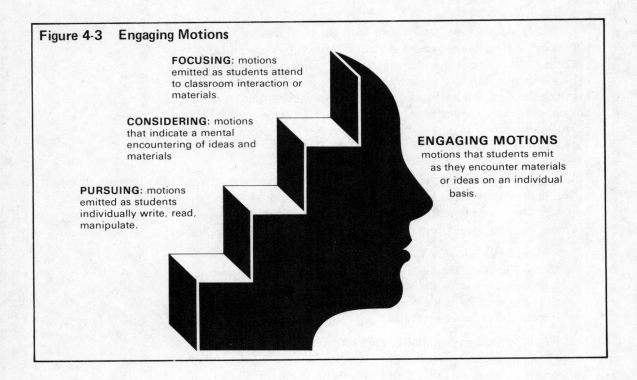

Figure 4-3   Engaging Motions

FOCUSING: motions emitted as students attend to classroom interaction or materials.

CONSIDERING: motions that indicate a mental encountering of ideas and materials

PURSUING: motions emitted as students individually write, read, manipulate.

ENGAGING MOTIONS motions that students emit as they encounter materials or ideas on an individual basis.

materials. A student's overt, noncontributing response to classroom interaction may be writing, reading, or manipulating materials. For instance, a student considers when he jots ideas in a notebook in response to a teacher's statement. Similarly, the student emits considering motions when he fills in a listening guide as an immediate response to class discussion, manipulates a pencil to complete a mathematics problem, writes down dictated spelling words. These motions are immediate responses to a teacher or student directive given in a group situation.

Pursuing Bernice sits at her desk working independently on a series of mathematics problems. Others have chosen to work in teams, but Bernice prefers to work by herself. She points to problems, checks previous examples, writes, erases, turns pages. She is actively engaged in learning tasks but in ways that do not involve her with others.

Bernice's actions can be termed *pursuing motions*. These are motions generally associated with the acts of writing down, reading, and manipulating when these acts are performed individually. For example, students emit pursuing motions when they

> pound the paper to get the paste to stick
> follow lines of print in a story they are reading to themselves
> flip passages in a dictionary to check a spelling

Although these actions may have been stimulated by some teacher directive, the motions are not an immediate response. In short, students are working on their own.

In classrooms structured informally, pursuing motions may occur under social conditions; a student may be conversing socially with a neighbor while each student works individually on a project. Their conversation, however, is a social one, unrelated to the project work.

Focusing, Considering, Pursuing   Information gleaned from analysis of students' engaging motions is highly significant. Engaging motions supply clues as to whether attention is being feigned. Focusing, considering, and pursuing motions are easy to fake. A student can lean forward as if attending assiduously; yet this motion can be part of a front purposefully constructed to impress the teacher. However, the teacher who knows the typical engaging patterns of his students may be able to sense when focusing and considering motions are not totally genuine. The clue may be a slightly different look in the student's eyes, a different posture. In some cases, it may be an exaggerated leaning or an heightened stillness of the body. Whatever the clue, if a teacher perceives the real message, he can change the level, tone, or pace of the interaction or simply open the windows to clear the air.

Charles Galloway makes an identical point about pursuing motions:

It has been discovered in viewing video tapes that some students deceive the teacher in their use of time. A prime example of this was seen with a third-grade girl who was a nonreader. For twenty minutes she went through the motions of being busy (during study time). She sharpened her pencil, moved her tablet around on the surface of the desk, looked at a book, etc., but did no work. Until she saw the video tape, the teacher believed the girl was "trying very hard" and "using her time profitably."[1]

---

1. Charles Galloway, *Teaching Is Communicating: Nonverbal Language in the Classroom* (Washington, D.C.: Association for Student Teaching, 1970), p. 10. Copyright 1970 by Association for Student Teaching; reprinted by permission of the publisher.

Galloway's example suggests that the teacher should consider whether a student's pursuing motions are genuine or whether they are time fillers resulting from inability to do or disinterest in the task.

Analysis of engaging motions, in addition, can supply the teacher with a clue as to the effectiveness of his instruction. Pursuing motions supply feedback as to the clarity of directions given and to the preparation of students for carrying out the task. Halting motions, false starts, turning to see how others are working may indicate that students do not understand. Their pursuing motions may signal a need for further explanation, more individual or small group assistance. Considering motions can similarly communicate: "I get it," "I don't like that," "You're going too fast," "I'm bored," "I'm waiting," "Repeat that."

"I can't hear" or "I can't see" are comparable messages that focusing motions send. The stretching of the neck or squint of the eyes may be a clue that the volume of interaction must be raised or that materials need to be displayed more prominently.

One way to handle nonverbal feedback is to watch the reaction of "barometer students"—students of average interest, ability, and attention who show their feelings clearly on their faces and through their bodies. The motions of these key students tell the teacher whether the message is coming across. A look of puzzlement from a barometer student signals that a message missed its mark. Full attention of key students signals success.

As this short section suggests, it is vital for a teacher to perceive engaging motions. Focusing, considering, and pursuing are "silent" motions—they lack a verbal accompaniment. The body sends the total message. When the teacher is unreceptive to engaging motions, his knowledge of student reaction is limited.

Activities for Analyzing Engaging Motions

1. Identify engaging motions emitted by students in a classroom in which you are observing or on a videotape you are watching. On the recording chart on page 61, list specific motions you observe that fall into each category.

2. Focus on nonverbal pursuing motions emitted by students.

   a. Look for actions signaling possible learning difficulties: the slow reader who moves his lips or points to each word as he reads silently; the reader who brings his book close or leans down toward his work (a vision problem?); the writer who clutches his pencil knuckle-fashion.

EXAMPLES OF ENGAGING MOTIONS		
Focusing	*Considering*	*Pursuing*

b. Observe the manner in which a student pursues. Consider whether the student is purposeful and definite; is hesitant; tends to use one series of motions or erases, stops, and repeats; pursues slowly or rapidly; uses motions as time-fillers to give the appearance of work.

c. Watch for nonverbal clues that communicate the intensity of a student's interest. Plot your inferences in chart form:

Determination   High ┕━━━━━━┷━━━━━━━┷━━━━━━┷━━━━━━┙ Low

Concentration   High ┕━━━━━━┷━━━━━━━┷━━━━━━┷━━━━━━┙ Low

Care about doing a   High ┕━━━━━━┷━━━━━━━┷━━━━━━┷━━━━━━┙ Low
    thorough job

d. Identify the tasks the student pursues successfully alone. Is it only when working with reading materials that the student takes a long time to settle down and makes many extraneous motions? Are the same motions evident when the student is writing, manipulating, drawing?

3. Project an overall profile of the engaging motions of a student in your classroom whom you consider to be a "barometer person." Simply note in the appropriate boxes the motions the student tends to repeat:

ENGAGING PATTERN OF _____

Focusing	Considering	Pursuing
Kinds of activities on which he focuses:	Characteristic considering gestures	Manner of pursuing:
Characteristic focusing motions:	Characteristic facial expressions:	Activities pursued intently:
Length of attention span:		Activities pursued with little intensity:

4. As you watch children and youth at different grade levels emit engaging motions, draw some general conclusions about how these motions differ from grade level to grade level.

THE LANGUAGE OF BEING

Motions categorized within the language of being are of five kinds: self-adjusting, nonattending, distracting, socializing, and facilitating.[2] In contrast to the language of participation, being motions have more to do with child's or youth's normal functioning as a human being than with his role as student.

Figure 4-4   The Language of Being

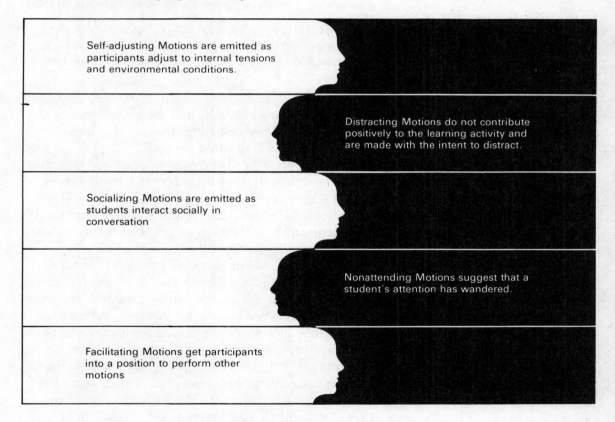

Self-adjusting Motions are emitted as participants adjust to internal tensions and environmental conditions.

Distracting Motions do not contribute positively to the learning activity and are made with the intent to distract.

Socializing Motions are emitted as students interact socially in conversation

Nonattending Motions suggest that a student's attention has wandered.

Facilitating Motions get participants into a position to perform other motions

---

2. Self-adjusting and facilitating categories are derived from the category system of teacher nonverbal activity presented in Barbara M. Grant, "A Method for Analyzing the Non-verbal Behavior (Physical Motions) of Teachers of Elementary School Language Arts." Unpublished doctoral dissertation. Teachers College, Columbia University, 1969.

Self-adjusting Motions

Students are human beings who itch, sneeze, have trouble with clothing, get restless. As a result of these human problems, they emit motions through which they adjust to internal conditions as well as to environmental variables affecting their well-being. For example, Bruce, a third grader, was observed emitting the following sequence of motions as he focused on the teacher who was reading a story. The boy

put his finger to his mouth, chewed his nail, put his finger down, clasped his hands together, made a shifting motion in his chair, peered at his hands, looked out the window, raised his left hand to his mouth, chewed his finger nail, looked around the room, lowered his hand, clasped his hands together, put one hand upward as a supporting brace, leaned his head on that hand, lowered his arm, folded his arms, unfolded his arms, lifted an arm again to serve as a head brace, leaned his head on hand, lowered that arm, shifted his feet, raised his arm, wiped his hand across his mouth, put finger in his mouth, chewed nails, shifted feet again, moved sideward in his chair, picked up pencil with other hand.

During this time, he conveyed the impression of thinking about the story—which he probably was. If Bruce had been asked to describe his motions, he would have had difficulty; he was more aware of the story than of his own self-adjusting motions.

Young children rarely keep their bodies motionless in periods of listening. Watch children who are attending to a discussion or demonstration. It is almost impossible to list every motion of a child. Observations in classrooms suggest that young children emit far more self-adjusting motions than do young adolescents, although adolescents emit numerous self-adjusting motions as well.

Self-adjusting motions are produced in reaction to tensions arising from the internal or external environment in which a person is interacting. When anyone sits too long, he gets restless; everyone has experienced the driving need to change position. Fatigue, too, can breed self-adjusting motions; the person leans his body against a support. Physical elements within the environment similarly can stimulate body motion: a fly settling on one's nose, light streaming into one's eyes, an uncomfortable temperature. The clothing one wears—a too-tight shoe, a binding belt, a loose button—can produce the same effect.[3] Motions elicited in response to these stimuli are

3. B. Grant and D. Hennings, *The Teacher Moves* (New York: Teachers College Press, 1971), pp. 10-11.

not generated by students as a form of misbehaving. In many instances, a self-adjusting motion is so much a part of a person that
the motion has become a mannerism.

Although self-adjusting motions may be outside the emitter's
awareness, they are some of the most telling clues a teacher can
listen for in his classroom. Self-adjusting motions can serve as
signals of brewing restlessness; though some restlessness is expected
from young people, growing restlessness from a number of barometer
students signals a need for change.

An almost complete cessation of body motion says something
too—because it is so uncommon. "Body quiet" can signal complete
student involvement. But as with all motion, quiet must be interpreted within the situational context. For instance, after students
have participated actively in a game of volley ball, body quiet may
signal physical exhaustion.

When a teacher fails to read the messages transmitted by self-
adjusting motions, students may invent excuses to stretch their
legs, release tensions, or rest from excessive activity; they go for a
drink, visit the rest rooms, or adjust the blinds. One young man
devised an ingenious way to handle his mounting tensions. He
would drop his pencil off the front of his desk, stand up, walk
around behind his chair and the front of his desk, pick up his
pencil, walk on around, and return to his seat. His teacher, interpreting his motions as self-adjusting, said nothing.

Teachers do modify their classroom activity in response to
increased restlessness read from student body talk. Sedentary
activities are interspersed with physical involvement. Discussion and
listening activities are limited to short periods—the exact time
block determined by students' overt self-adjusting motions. The
teacher keeps moving so that students must vary their focus if they
are to continue watching an operation in progress.

Similarly, teachers recognize individual differences in students'
restlessness quotients. One youngster may be able to engage for
long periods of time, emitting few self-adjusting motions that spell
restlessness. In contrast, a second student may emit self-adjusting
motions after only a short period of engaging motions. Such differences suggest the need to provide different scheduling sequences
for students based on signals received from self-adjusting motions.

Not only restlessness and tiredness but anger, fear, caring,
nervousness are communicated by self-adjusting motions. Recently

a government official testified before a congressional hearing on an executive action that had been ill-received by Congress; he was on the hot seat! Watching the official on the evening news, this author was impressed by the man's smiling countenance, evenness of words, and calmness of body. But that he was irritated was evident in his neck. He swallowed repeatedly as he waited to respond; his neck muscles were taut. To understand the man's feelings, the listener had to go beyond superficial signs of calm that the speaker had taught himself to emit and focus on less obvious signs.

With students, especially young persons who have taught themselves to put on a brave front, the teacher needs to look for the subtle message. Motions indicative of fear, nervousness, and anger can be masked under a deceptively calm exterior, but physical signs of tension, changes in color and body moisture can still communicate beneath the calm. A student's flush or pallor, beads of perspiration can "say" that a youngster finds the situation disturbing.

Nonattending Motions

All teachers know that students are not always attentive. Although Bruce, the boy previously described, was generally attentive to the story, his attention wandered. For just a moment he glanced out the window. A few minutes later, a bell rang somewhere in the school, and he glanced at the clock. But for Bruce, these were short lapses signaled to the teacher by his wandering eyes and the change in body orientation. In contrast, a student may stare into space for long periods lost in thought, may focus extendedly on something that is not the center of group activity, or may fall asleep.

Nonattending motions generally are not distracting to others unless, of course, the motions are carried to extreme or the teacher calls attention to them. They are emitted by the student without intent to distract; the student simply finds something more interesting or begins to dream. Actually, behavior problems often originate in a teacher's inability to read messages sent by self-adjusting and nonattending body language and to change the classroom environment eliciting these motions. The teacher who continues a sedentary activity when numbers of students are nonverbally signaling inattention is asking for trouble.

Students differ in ability to attend. Some students can attend to a discussion for only a short time before they begin to emit nonattending motions. The younger child generally exhibits non-attending motions more quickly than older students; the hyper-active child, similarly, falls into this category. In both instances, active involvement is imperative if nonattending motions are to be kept to a minimum.

Distracting Motions

Some student motions are emitted with intent to distract others. For example, a student may

> strike another youngster with a pencil
> make faces
> drop his book intentionally
> poke another participant
> make "crazy" hand gestures

These motions are generally frowned upon. Some endanger others. As a result, the motions attract attention.

Interpreting distracting motions is difficult, for essentially the teacher is determining intent. For instance, a boy is swinging the venetian blind cord; over and over again he swings that cord until the teacher is driven to desperation. But is that boy swinging sub-consciously in reaction to general restlessness and without aware-ness of his actions? Or is he swinging deliberately to annoy? Know-ledge of the student's characteristic ways of operating—the facial expressions and gesture patterns he uses when he sets out deliberately to upset—is requisite if one is to interpret the meaning of the motion.

Sometimes the teacher's ego-involvement prevents an accurate interpretation. The notion that a teacher should run a well-disci-plined classroom has been so ingrained in a teacher that he may auto-matically interpret the youth's self-adjusting motions as a distraction. The teacher immediately assumes that the youth is defiant and as a result makes an issue from what may be a simple self-adjusting motion.

Socializing Motions

Schools of the 1970s are far different from schools of the past. Children in open classrooms communicate informally with one another as they go about individual tasks. It is not uncommon to see two students working diligently on their individual art projects, written compositions, or translation exercises while at the same time encountering one another on a social basis. A girl leans over to chat momentarily with a friend, makes laughing motions as she speaks, smiles companionably, or even pauses to write down a time when she will meet her friend out of school. In some classrooms in which socializing within clearly defined limits is encouraged, none of these motions is considered a distraction; they are accepted as part of the language of socialization that people naturally speak.

This, of course, makes categorizing nonverbal language a difficult task for an outsider; how a motion is interpreted depends on the limits of acceptable behavior established in the classroom, not on an outside observer's expectation of how a classroom should be run. If the teacher considers a motion as distracting, that may well be what it is. After all, the teacher's concept of what "goes" in the classroom sets the boundaries of acceptable motion within the classroom.

The nonverbal language of socialization spoken in classrooms tells a teacher much about existing interpersonal relationships and the success or failure of students to form new relationships. With young children, the motions of socialization are easy to observe. Two little girls join hands as they walk down the corridor; their bodies move in unison as they giggle over a shared confidence; they move into seats next to one another when given a chance to choose. Boys speak their own language of socialization: they run to stand next to each other in line, often with some shoving and pushing; they glance sideward at each other as they wait in line; they huddle in secret conversation. Older students, in contrast, emit more subtle socialization motions.

Facilitating Motions

In order to pursue an activity, people must transport themselves from one location to another. In order to carry out certain tasks, they must move parts of their bodies, move materials, or move other people. Specifically, they must walk toward a bookcase before they can scan a title and take down a book. They must lean down to pick something up, open a book if they want to read it. This is the inherent nature of movement.

In classrooms, facilitating motions are, of course, seen continually. A student

> walks toward the shelf to get paper
>
> lifts an arm to write on the board
>
> turns in the seat to hand paper to the next student

Such facilitating motions through which students change position in space generally occur in concert or in a series with other motions. When a student raises an arm to scratch, or walks to the front of the room to write a contribution on the board, or reaches into a desk for paper, these motions facilitate other activities.

To relegate facilitating motions to a position of unimportance would be an error. A popular song of several years ago tells us that

> There's a kind of walk you walk when you're walking happy,
> There's a kind of walk you walk when you're walking sad.[4]

The way a person carries out facilitating motions often tells how that person feels. In the words of the song: Is the student "walking happy"? Is his step light and bouncy? Are body muscles relaxed? Or is the student "walking sad"? Is he dragging his feet? Do shoulders speak of dejection?

Facilitating motions vary, too, in speed. Some participants normally move quickly: they dart into place, yank out materials, jerk their bodies. Other students move more slowly: they saunter into place and dawdle as they prepare materials. Still others move with a deliberateness and attention to detail that even carries over to the way they walk. Viewed within this context, any major changes in characteristic speed of motion can have meaning.

In like manner, facilitating motions vary in ease of execution. The young adolescent who is experiencing a growth spurt in which some parts of his body seem to grow faster than other parts has an awkwardness that can prove an annoyance to the teacher who has not perceived this as a natural feature of that young person's motion pattern. The youth appears to stumble, knock over things far beyond reach, and drop objects he is carrying. The teacher, who finds that the stumble comes just at a key moment and interrupts the

---

4. From "Walking Happy," words by Sammy Cahn, music by James Van Heusen. Shapiro, Bernstein & Co., Inc., 1962, 1966.

sequence of events, may be tempted to reprimand, thinking that the youth stumbles intentionally. In some instances, awkwardness may be intentional to gain attention and make fun. But possible too is the explanation that awkwardness is an integral part of the youth's facilitating motions.

Analyzing Being Motions

1. As you observe a lesson on site or on videotape, identify motions that could be classified as the language of being. List specific motions.

EXAMPLES OF BEING MOTIONS				
Self-adjusting	*Nonattending*	*Distracting*	*Socializing*	*Facilitating*

2. What evidence do you perceive that indicates a teacher is adjusting his teaching to the nonverbal feedback received via being motions of students. Describe specific incidents.
3. Develop a profile of a student's typical language of being.

BEING PROFILE OF _____ _____

Self-adjusting Motions

Characteristic motions:

Conditions under which motions tend to
appear:

Nonattending Motions

Characteristic motions:

Conditions under which motions tend to
appear:

Ways of restoring attention:

Distracting Motions

Characteristic motions:

Conditions under which motions tend to
appear:

Socializing Motions

Characteristic motions:

Manner in which motions are emitted:

Facilitating Motions

Characteristics of motion:
    Ease
    Speed
    Productivity of

4. Watch for subtle signs of fear, nervousness, anger—self-adjust-
    ing motions that older students may try to mask. Describe
    classroom episodes that suggest a masking effect.

5. As you observe in a lower-grade class, list all self-adjusting
    motions produced by a youngster during a four-minute period;
    then switch your observations to a second youngster for
    another four minutes, then to a third for another four minutes.
    Do the same as you observe at higher grade levels. What con-
    clusions can you draw about the comparative use of self-
    adjusting motions at different grade levels? What implications
    do your conclusions have for instructional strategies?

THE LANGUAGE OF HEIGHTENING

As a person communicates, he uses body language as a natural
accompaniment to spoken words. This body music—so to speak—
helps clarify and emphasize. Barbara Grant has classified such body
language as emitted by teachers into three categories: emphasizing,
illustrating, and pantomiming.[5] Since these kinds of motions are
common to all communication, these categories can be applied to
student motion as well. They are what herein is called the language
of heightening.

Emphasizing Motions

As suggested by Albert Scheflen in *Body Language and Social Order*,
"some gestures are used as indicators of stress" as when a man
punches his own palm to be emphatic.[6] Tactile gestures and facial
gestures can similarly be used to say, "This is important."[7]

    Of course, since emphasizing motions are an integral part of
speaking, tactile, facial, and hand gestures are emitted frequently
by students in classrooms. Giving a report, a girl moves her hands
expressively at certain points to suggest greater stress; her body
moves rhythmically to accompany her words. At other times,
students use stronger emphasizing gestures. The girl who is absolutely certain may pound the desk resoundingly as she says, "I know
it's right."

---

5. Grant, *op. cit.*, p. 43.
6. Albert Scheflen, *Body Language and Social Order* (Englewood Cliffs, N.J.: Prentice-Hall, 1972), p. 41.
7. *Ibid.*, pp. 44, 45.

Figure 4-5   The Language of Heightening

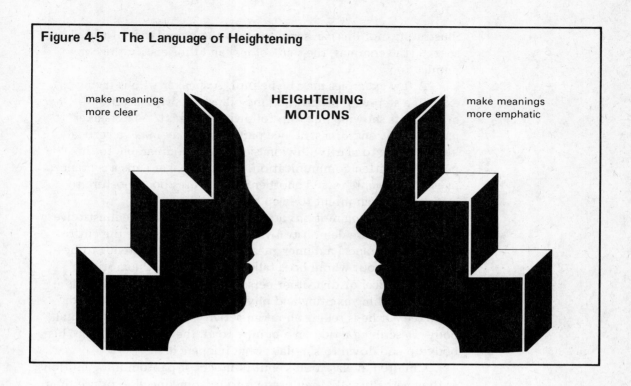

make meanings
more clear

**HEIGHTENING
MOTIONS**

make meanings
more emphatic

Students differ in the amount of motion they emit as an emphasizing accompaniment to their verbal speech. Some people are highly active; their bodies are particularly expressive. Others are considerably more passive; their facial expressions communicate little about how they feel as they speak, they attempt only infrequent tactile communication with others as a means of emphasizing, and they physically gesture with only limited portions of their bodies. We might call the latter type *nonverbally oriented communicants.*

Clarifying Motions

Clarifying motions serve a variety of purposes. According to Scheflen, "a speaker's gestures may refer to objects or persons about whom he is speaking." Demonstrative gestures are used to indicate size and shape, to clarify an abstraction by making a concrete picture with hands or body. Furthermore, what Grant classes as illustrating motions can serve to mark the boundaries of verbal speech (the commas, the semicolons) and thus clarify the communication.[8]

A few examples may be helpful. A speaker who is trying to explain a step-wise progression may illustrate with a series of movements showing one step following the next. As a speaker pauses at the end of a sentence pattern, he may make a vertical kinesic move to clarify; the kinesic move is comparable to the period in written communication. Or if a speaker ends a sentence, pauses, but wants to add another idea, he uses body posture to communicate an intent to keep speaking.

Pantomiming motions are an extension of simple illustrative motions; they are demonstrative gestures that involve the entire body. For instance, a dinner guest for a moment pretends to be the person about whom he is talking; he assumes the motion patterns typical of that other person. At another point, he tells about something exciting and physically describes the event for all to see. Or he is telling about an activity that involves the total body. Describing a ride on a bumpy road, the speaker bounces his body up and down to simulate what happened.

Children in classrooms emit numbers of pantomiming motions; as they verbally talk, they pretend to be someone else, or use their bodies in uninhibited fashion to simulate a motion or an emotion previously experienced. Classroom observations suggest that younger children emit pantomiming motions much more often than do students in upper grades.

Analyzing Heightening Motions

1. Identify specific heightening motions emitted by students in a classroom you are observing in fact or on videotape. List these motions in chart fashion. On your chart, star those motions you believe to be pantomiming motions. How does the number of pantomiming motions compare with the number of other illustrating motions emitted during the same time period?

---

8. Albert Scheflen, *Body Language and Social Order*, pp. 42-43, 46-51.

EXAMPLES OF HEIGHTENING MOTIONS	
Emphasizing Motions	*Clarifying Motions*

2. As you observe classroom interaction, study the manner in which kinesic moves are used to "punctuate" conversation. How does a particular speaker "say" that he is pausing only momentarily and intends to continue? "say" that he is finished and expects the teacher to respond? punctuate linguistic questions with kinesic moves? What kinesic accompaniment does he employ to punctuate linguistic exclamations?
3. If you are interested in pursuing what Scheflen has called *the markers of speech*, read Chapter 3 of *Body Language and Social Order*, Prentice-Hall, 1972.
4. You may want to map a specific student's heightening motions.

Heightening Motions of _____

Emphasizing
Characteristic emphasizing gestures

Clarifying
Characteristic illustrating gestures

5. Based on the profile you map in activity 4, draw conclusions about the typical motion pattern of the student:

   a. Does the student appear more active physically as he talks than do other children in the class?
   b. Does the student tend to rely on words to transmit thoughts? have a verbal orientation toward communication?
   c. Does the student have a basic set of gestures (a repertoire) that are repeated? Does he repeat any motions to the extent that they are annoying to a listener?
   d. Does the student use facial expressions as part of his heightening repertoire? tactile gestures?
   e. Does the student use large-sized gestures as accompaniment to verbal speech? Does he restrict gesturing to small motions?
   f. Does the student use kinesic motion effectively to punctuate verbal speech? Are his motions open to misinterpretation?

6. Study the way a teacher interprets the kinesic punctuation emitted by students in his class. What evidence can you compile indicating that the teacher is aware of and responding to these clarifying motions? In contrast, what evidence can you compile indicating lack of awareness on the teacher's part?

7. As you teach, try to concentrate on the kinesic punctuation of students. Consider whether you tend to overlook kinesic signals and interrupt students who are clearly signaling they are not finished talking.

8. After leading a discussion session, rethink (or review on video-tape) the sequence of activities to determine if you were aware of and responding to the kinesic messages sent by students.

    a. What was the nature of students' nonverbal participation in the discussion?
    b. What was the extent of the students' joining motions?
    c. What evidence do you have that students were considering ideas under discussion?
    d. What evidence do you have that students were focusing on materials and other participants? Do you think some of the focusing behavior was being feigned?
    e. What self-adjusting motions were you aware of? did you respond to? Did any of these motions disturb you?
    f. What nonattending motions were you aware of? did you respond to?
    g. How did you handle the kinesic punctuation of students? How many times did you interrupt when a student had signaled intent to continue?
    h. Did the emphasizing motions of students indicate a high (or low) level of student involvement in the discussion?
    i. Did the clarifying motions of students suggest to you that students were beginning to get a clear concept of the topic under discussion?

9. After organizing and guiding an independent work period, think about what was being "told" to you nonverbally during the session.

    a. Did the nonverbal activity of barometer students indicate that students generally knew how to handle their tasks?
    b. Were there some children whose nonverbal activity indicated that they were copying from others?
    c. Were any students emitting time-filling motions to pretend involvement?
    d. What evidence do you have indicating that students were enjoying their work?
    e. How did students signal to you that they were finished with the task?
    f. Did the attention of students wander from the task? How do you know?
    g. During the work period, did any students simultaneously make socializing motions? Did the socializing motions occupy more time than the pursuing motions?
    h. During the session, what nonverbal calls for help did you respond to?
    i. Did the motions of the students indicate that they were rushing to complete the task in the stipulated time?

10. It is possible to do a comprehensive analysis of all student motions emitted during a unit of time. To do this, of course, requires a videotaped recording of motions emitted. For anyone who wants to try to do this as a way of studying motions over small units of time, the category system described in Module 4 is given in Figure 4.6. Remember that the system was developed to serve as a practical guide to the teacher rather than as a highly reliable research instrument. Therefore, conclusions you draw about numbers and kinds of motions should be considered tentative.

Figure 4.6   A Guide for Analyzing Student Nonverbal Language

1.0	**The Language of Participation**—body language emitted as students encounter the learning activities of a classroom.
1.1	*Contributing Motions*—motions that make a direct contribution to a group learning activity and that are focused on by others who are participating in the activity.
	Joining motions—motions that indicate a desire to contribute actively or to work with someone else in a learning activity,
	Expressing motions—motions emitted as a joiner contributes substantively in a discussion-type situation and nonverbally expresses meanings related to the learning activity.
	Performing motions—motions emitted as a joiner participates in nondiscussion, presentational activities in which motions do not serve as a model for how-to-do-it; for example, motions produced as part of a sports event, an exhibition, a dramatic activity, a unison-type activity.
	Demonstrating motions—motions emitted as a joiner participates in presentational activities in which motions serve as a model for how-to-do-it.
	Helping motions—motions emitted as a participant carries out house-keeping chores necessary to the maintenance of the overall group activity.
1.2	*Engaging Motions*—learning-related motions that do not contribute directly to the learning of others and are not the focus of other participants' attention.
	Focusing motions—motions suggesting that a student is attending to interaction, performances, demonstrations, and the like, without being actively involved with others and without being the focus of others' attention.
	Considering motions—motions suggesting that a student is actively thinking about ideas or materials being presented in an interaction, demonstration, performance, or the like.
	Pursuing motions—motions emitted as a student works independently on the problems and/or materials of learning without reference to an ongoing discussion, demonstration, or performance; specifically, motions typical of independent study activity.

Figure 4.6   A Guide for Analyzing Student Nonverbal Language (continued)

2.0	**The Language of Being**—body language arising from a participant's self-adjusting activity, non-attending activity, attempts to distract and socialize, and facilitating activities; motions through which a student interjects his "humanness" into the situation.
2.1	*Self-adjusting Motions*—motions emitted as a participant adjusts to internal tensions and environmental conditions that affect his well-being.
2.2	*Nonattending Motions*—motions suggesting a student's attention has wandered from the learning activity; these motions are not made deliberately to distract others in the situation.
2.3	*Distracting Motions*—motions not contributing positively to the learning activity and made with the intent to distract.
2.4	*Socializing Motions*—motions through which participants interact socially in conversation not related to the learning activity.
2.5	*Facilitating Motions*—motions that make possible other motions, that get the participant into a position to perform other motions.
3.0	**The Language of Heightening**—body language through which meanings are made more emphatic and/or explicit and that is an integral part of the communication of meanings.
3.1	*Emphasizing Motions*—physical motions that indicate the importance of meanings being considered.
3.2	*Clarifying Motions*—illustrating and pantomiming motions that make ideas, things, or persons more clear and concrete; also motions that regulate communication among participants.

NOTE: Self-adjusting, facilitating, and heightening motions are derived from the Grant system for analyzing nonverbal activity of teachers; see Grant and Hennings, *The Teacher Moves* (Teachers College Press, 1971).

The teacher gains competency in—

analyzing the amount of student talk occurring in a classroom and distinguishing between student statements that represent a response or an initiation

distinguishing between student talk that is learning-related and that is non-learning-related

distinguishing between statements representing student recall and statements representing higher levels of thinking

interpreting what students say in terms of the thought processes represented by student statements

describing the work of linguists who explain nonstandard dialects in terms of a difference model; hopefully, the teacher will become more accepting of the language patterns of nonstandard speakers and reflect this in his teaching

MODULE 5
Listening for
Student Verbal
Messages

Continuing research on verbal classroom interaction provides the teacher with techniques and category systems for studying the verbal statements of students. Many of the systems designed within the past ten years are highly reliable means for analyzing classroom interaction if used with the precision described by investigators. Even if used informally without the related mathematical and technical coding procedures, these systems can supply the teacher and the teacher-in-training with knowledge about teaching strategies and the overall pattern of verbal interaction in the classroom.

LISTENING TO STUDENT TALK

One kind of information that analysis of verbal interaction can supply is knowledge about who does the talking in the classroom. According to Ned A. Flanders, statements that occur in the classroom can be categorized in one of three major classes: (1) teacher talk, (2) student talk, and (3) silence or confusion, used to handle anything else that is not teacher or student talk.[1] Based on his experimental data, Flanders contends that two thirds of the time someone is talking in the typical classroom; two thirds of that talk is emitted by the teacher.[2]

The Flanders category system can be applied easily during firsthand classroom observation or videotape study of discussion

---

1. Ned A. Flanders, *Analyzing Teaching Behavior* (Reading, Mass.: Addison-Wesley, 1970), pp. 33-34. Copyright 1970 by Addison-Wesley; described by permission of the publisher.
2. Edmund J. Amidon and Ned A. Flanders, *The Role of the Teacher in the Classroom* (Minneapolis, Minn.: Paul S. Amidon & Associates, Inc., 1963), p. 44.

periods in which the teacher and several students participate. The observer counts out one second, two seconds, three seconds and then marks a tally in the appropriate box of a recording guide, tallying in the "T" box if the teacher is speaking verbally, in the "St" box if a student is speaking verbally, and in the "S" box if there is general verbal silence or if it is impossible to tell who is speaking. As soon as the observer has indicated the active speaker, he counts another three seconds, and records again.

If this procedure is continued for approximately five minutes and several five-minute periods are studied, the result will be a series of tallies in each of the blocks. The observer can determine the percentage of talk contributed by students and by the teacher as shown in Figure 5-1 and can determine whether the teacher is

	Tallies Recorded at 3-second intervals	Total tallies in Each Category	Total Tallies Representing Talk
Teacher talk T	ⅢⅢ ⅢⅢ ⅢⅢ ⅢⅢ ⅢⅢ ⅢⅢ ⅢⅢ ⅢⅢ ⅢⅢ ⅢⅢ ⅢⅢ ⅢⅢ ⅢⅢ	65	85
Student talk St	ⅢⅢ ⅢⅢ ⅢⅢ ⅢⅢ	20	
Silence or confusion S	ⅢⅢ ⅢⅢ ⅢⅢ ⅢⅢ ⅢⅢ	25	
	Total Tallies Recorded	110	

Figure 5-1
A Recording Guide for Analyzing Student Talk

Percentage student talk = 20/85 X 100 = 23.5 percent
Percentage teacher talk = 65/85 X 100 = 76.5 percent
Percentage of total time spent in talk = 85/110 X 100 = 77 percent

Conclusion: In this time period, the amount of student talk was considerably less than the average found by Flanders.

approaching Flanders' approximation of 33.33 percent student talk to 66.67 percent teacher talk. Of course, this proportion is the average—not the ideal. The teacher must decide whether the amount of student talk gives students sufficient opportunity to react to information, to explain, to relate, to infer. This is a value judgment.

In the Flanders system, student talk is further subdivided into *responses* and *initiations*. Statements that answer a teacher question or directive are considered responses; they are emitted at the prompting of the teacher. In contrast, statements emitted without teacher prompting—when a student asks a question or expresses a thought not asked for by the teacher—are considered initiations.[3]

Student talk that is either a response-to-teacher or an initiation typify contributions in teacher-led discussions. On the other hand, in more open discussion situations, students answer questions posed by other students; and students serve as moderators of discussions in which teachers take a back seat. A third kind of student talk occurs here: the response to another student's query. Adding this category to Flanders' system, the observer has three categories for studying student talk: response to teacher, response to student, and initiation. Figure 5-2 indicates how to calculate the kinds of student talk occurring in a classroom after the observer has classified and tallied each student statement emitted during a time period.

Because this modified Flanders system has only three categories, it can be kept in mind by a teacher involved in classroom discussion. As students speak, the teacher informally categorizes student statements: "Joe is responding to my question." "Tim is raising a question; Tim generally does raise questions." "Mark is responding to Tim's question." From this type of informal consideration, the teacher-in-action can gain some general notions about the student talk emitted in the classroom.

The Flanders system—which in actuality is much more sophisticated than so far described in this section—was designed as a research instrument to determine the amount of freedom a teacher grants to students. The information supplied by study of the response/initiation pattern does provide a clue. The classroom in which student talk is limited to responses to the teacher is probably one in which children or young people are given little freedom to initiate ideas; conversely, the classroom in which students actively respond to

---

3. Flanders, *loc. cit.*

	Tallies of Student Statements	Total Tallies in Each Category
Responses to Teacher r/t	⦶⧄ ⦶⧄ ⦶⧄ ⦶⧄ ⦶⧄ /	26
Responses to Other Students r/st	///	3
Initiations i	⦶⧄ ///	8
	Total Tallies Recorded	37

Figure 5-2
A Recording Guide
for Analyzing Kinds
of Student Talk

Percentage of student talk that is *r/t* = 26/37 X 100 = 70 percent

Percentage of student talk that is *r/st* = 3/37 X 100 = 8 percent

Percentage of student talk that is *i* = 8/37 X 100 = 22 percent

This chart shows that 70 percent of all student verbal expressions were responses to the teacher, during the time period under investigation.

other students and initiate may be one in which students are encouraged to share thoughts with one another, raise questions, and give directions.

Of course, the experienced teacher knows that another factor can account for high student initiation and student-to-student response: an explosive disciplinary situation in which students call out inappropriate remarks and talk socially among themselves while a total class discussion is in progress. The system for describing nonverbal behavior developed in Module 4 can help to show the percentage of student statements that are not related to the ongoing work of the class. Contributing motions and being motions have their corollaries in the verbal domain. *Contributing statements*—whether verbal or nonverbal—relate to the ongoing work of the class; we can say they are learning-related since they are emitted as students encounter the content and processes of the curriculum. *Being statements*, on the other hand, are related more directly to normal human functioning and relate less directly to learning processes; we can say they are non-learning-related. They are emitted as students socialize, adjust to inner tensions, attempt to disrupt.

An observer looking at student statements in a rather systematic way can modify the recording guide to distinguish between contributing statements and being statements; the three-box tally

Figure 5-3   Examples of Contributing and Being Statements of Students

"This heat is too much for me."

"Can't we take a break now?"

"I dropped my pencil."

"Your hair looks nice today."

"Are you going to the show tonight?"

BEING STATEMENTS

"Connect the thistle tube to the hose."

"Jelly fish can sting you till they leave welts"

"I think we shouldn't have sold the wheat to Russia."

"The 747 costs 29 million."

CONTRIBUTING STATEMENTS

guide is converted into a six-box guide as shown in Figure 5-4. From the tallies the observer can determine what percentage of student initiations and student-to-student responses are learning-related and non-learning-related. The teacher-in-action can carry out the same type of analysis more informally. As students initiate and respond, the teacher considers: "Jack is initiating—but not learning-related." "Tim's question is contributing to the learning."

**Figure 5-4
Recording the
Contributing
and Being
Statements of
Students**

Response to Teacher	Response to Student	Initiation	Totals
Contributing Statements ⫶⫶⫶⫶ ⫶⫶⫶⫶ ⫶⫶⫶⫶ ⫶⫶⫶⫶ //// 24	// 2	⫶⫶⫶⫶ / 6	32
Response to Teacher	**Response to Student**	**Initiation**	**Totals**
Being Statements // 2	/ 1	// 2	5

Percentage of being statements = 5/37 X 100 = 13.5 percent

Total	37

The teacher may also be interested in discovering the extent of active student involvement as well as in gaining some understanding of the kinds of statements that characterize a particular student's participation. Are all the initiations being emitted by a single student who perhaps is more venturesome than others? Do some students tend only to respond, rarely to initiate? A technique borrowed from sociologists who have studied patterns of group interaction can be helpful in this context. Draw a rough map of the classroom indicating with a circle the position of each student.

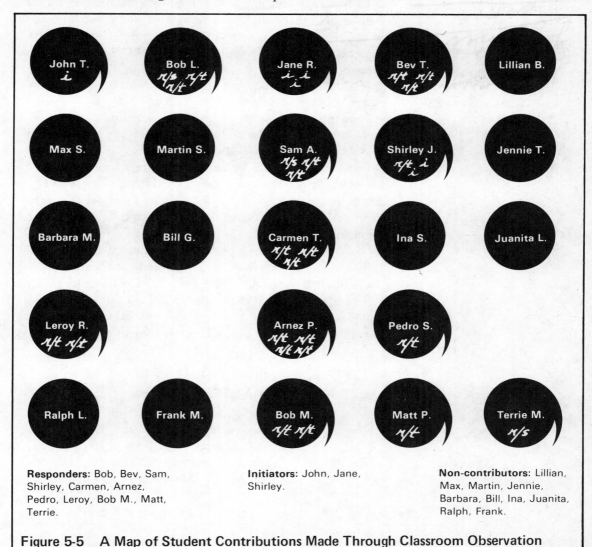

Responders: Bob, Bev, Sam, Shirley, Carmen, Arnez, Pedro, Leroy, Bob M., Matt, Terrie.

Initiators: John, Jane, Shirley.

Non-contributors: Lillian, Max, Martin, Jennie, Barbara, Bill, Ina, Juanita, Ralph, Frank.

Figure 5-5   A Map of Student Contributions Made Through Classroom Observation

Whenever a student responds to another student or to the teacher and whenever a student makes an initiatory statement, indicate that by placing *r/t*, *r/st*, or *i* in the circle representing him. In a classroom in which most of the student verbal behavior is response-to-teacher, this technique obviously produces little information; but in classes where student leadership in thinking does occur, the technique may provide additional insights about student talk.

Activities for Studying Student Talk

1. Listen to a tape recording of a classroom discussion you are leading. Then using the counting system described on page 81 and the recording guide depicted in Figure 5-1, figure out the percentage of talk contributed by students. If you observe in a classroom, carry out the recording on site. Consider the implications of the data you gather. Do you believe that the teacher is doing too much of the talking?

2. Analyze the nature of student talk by listening to the tape again. This time use the guide shown in Figure 5-2 and tally the statements that are response-to-teacher, response-to-student, and initiation. Calculate the percentage of student statements falling into each category. If you observe in a classroom, carry out the tallying on site. Consider the implications. Are students being encouraged to take a leadership role in the interaction?

3. As you teach, informally consider the amount and kinds of student talk emitted. Ask: "How often do students raise questions that contribute?" "How often do students volunteer to answer another student's query?" "Do I tend to do most of the talking?"

4. Classify the following statements as contributing or as being:

    _____ a. "Stop bothering me!"

    _____ b. "It's time for lunch."

    _____ c. "I think it is sulfur dioxide."

    _____ d. "Macbeth's wife was overliberated."

    _____ e. "I want a drink."

    _____ f. "Today war ends differently from the way war ended a few years ago."

    _____ g. "You're a bird brain."

a. being; *b.* being; *c.* contributing; *d.* contributing; *e.* being; *f.* contributing; *g.* being

5. Analyze an audiotape of a class session for the percentage of student statements that are contributing statements and the percentage that are being.
6. Numerically record the responses and initiations of all the students in a class during several segments of a discussion using a seating guide to record as shown in Figure 5-5. Identify the responders, the initiators, the noncontributors. Consider whether most of the active contributors are boys or girls.
7. Researchers find the order of student statements significant. Do students who respond go on to elaborate or raise additional questions? To study

teacher question ------► student response ------► student initiation

patterns, record in abbreviated fashion the teacher statement and the student response and initiation that followed as you listen to a tape of classroom discussion or to firsthand inter-action. Hypothesize what triggered the student to initiate. Listen for such sequences as you teach.

INTERPRETING LEVELS OF THINKING

Most present-day investigators of verbal classroom interaction have concerned themselves not only with the amount of student talk as compared with teacher talk and with the amount of student initiated talk but also with the intellectual operations represented by student statements. Arno Bellack in his investigations of verbal interaction in high school social science classrooms, Hilda Taba in her studies of interaction in elementary school social science class-rooms, and Benjamin Bloom in his analytical work that resulted in the taxonomy of objectives in the cognitive domain have all identi-fied intellectual processes that occur in classrooms.[4] The work of Bellack, Taba, Bloom, and others supplies the teacher with clear descriptions of cognitive processes; this work has been used as a theoretical base for the following classification of thinking repre-sented by student statements in classrooms.

Recalling

Much of what students state in classrooms represents what Benja-min Bloom calls "knowledge." Students emit specifics such as

---

4. Arno Bellack, *The Language of the Classroom* (New York: Teachers College Press, 1966); Hilda Taba, *Thinking in Elementary School Children.* Cooperative Research Project No. 1574 (San Francisco: San Francisco State College, 1964); Benjamin Bloom, *Taxonomy of Educational Objectives; The Classification of Educational Goals, Cognitive Domain* (New York: David McKay, 1956).

terms and facts, rules, procedures, definitions, lines of poetry and prose, generalizations that they have committed to memory. Because emitting knowledge requires simple recall of what one has previously been told or read, Benjamin Bloom considers repeating knowledge as the base level of human cognition.[5]

To determine whether a statement made by a student represents recall of knowledge, the teacher must consider the student's statement within the context in which it occurred. If the student responds to

a. "Who wrote *Much Ado About Nothing?*" with "Shakespeare," or
b. "Where is Ephesus?" with "Turkey," or
c. "Who succeeds an impeached President?" with "The Vice-President,"

the responses represent recall. Similarly, if the student responds to

d. "How do we punctuate items in a series?" with "a comma after each item," or
e. "What are the five classes of vertebrates?" with "Mammals, birds, reptiles, amphibians, fish," or
f. "What is Newton's First Law of Motion?" with "A body in motion will remain in motion unless another force is applied to change its state of motion,"

the student is recalling knowledge already assimilated.

Obviously, the answers to the above questions differ in the kinds of knowledge sought. The last answer is a statement of an involved generalization, whereas the first answer states a specific fact and the fourth is a statement of a rule. Nonetheless, each answer indicates only ability to repeat.

Although recall of knowledge is an essential base upon which to build higher levels of cognition, interaction in which most student statements represent recall has inherent weaknesses. Norris Sanders in *Classroom Questions: What Kinds?* identifies three limitations: the rate of forgetting is rapid; memorized knowledge does not necessarily represent a high level of understanding; and instruction that concentrates on recall neglects other significant intellectual operations.[6] These higher-level operations include reflecting, relating, projecting, valuing, and inventing.[7]

---

5. Bloom, *op. cit.*, p. 18.
6. Norris Sanders, *Classroom Questions: What Kinds?* (New York: Harper & Row, 1966), pp. 27-28.
7. Dorothy G. Hennings and Barbara Grant, *Content and Craft* (Englewood Cliffs, N.J.: Prentice-Hall, 1973), pp. 9-11.

Reflecting

Reflecting requires the thinker to go beyond recall to rephrase, summarize, or describe. It involves a person in translating ideas or firsthand observations into his own words.[8]

When students rephrase, they translate what they have heard or read into their own words; they paraphrase. To rephrase, they must "understand written or oral communication, for without ability to comprehend what one has read, one can hardly translate it faithfully."[9] That students who have "learned" something by memorizing may be unable to translate it into their own words is shown in the classic anecdote about the first-grade student who recited the Pledge of Allegiance each morning. When asked what the pledge meant, the student was speechless. The same lack of understanding of spoken words was shown by the elementary school child who was asked to draw a picture to tell about the Christmas song he was singing. The song was the one with the line "and a partridge in a pear tree." The youngster's picture showed a bullet (or cartridge) hanging in the tree.

Rephrasing often goes beyond simple paraphrasing to include summarizing. When students emit summarizing statements, they select what they consider to be the key elements of an event or communication and use those to tell about the event or communication in an abbreviated form. A student summarizes when he

tells the main points developed in a chapter
tells the key points discussed yesterday
gives a condensed version of what happened

In each case, the student is selecting significant elements, rejecting less significant elements, and in the process is offering proof of comprehension.

The student who describes based on direct observations is similarly functioning at a higher level than recall. When a student "reads" a picture and says, "The school bus is picking up the children. It's yellow. A boy is running toward the bus," the student is translating the details of the picture into a verbal description. The same intellectual process takes place when a student describes real-life things and events, such as the number of petals, sepals, stamens in a flower that he is examining.

---

8. Bloom, *op. cit.*, p. 91.
9. Hennings and Grant, *op. cit.*, p. 18.

These examples show the fundamental relationship that exists between knowledge and higher levels of cognition. To describe the picture, the child must know that the name of the vehicle in the picture is bus; to describe the flower specimen, the biology student must know which part is called sepal. In these contexts, the students are using knowledge—not just repeating it.

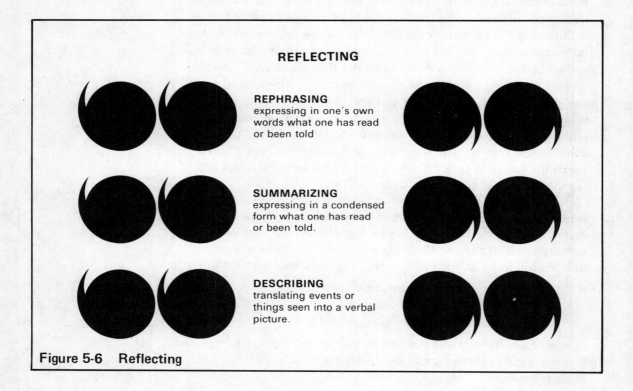

REFLECTING

REPHRASING
expressing in one's own words what one has read or been told

SUMMARIZING
expressing in a condensed form what one has read or been told.

DESCRIBING
translating events or things seen into a verbal picture.

Figure 5-6   Reflecting

Relating

A more sophisticated form of cognition is represented by student statements that propose relationships between two or more items or ideas. Students are doing more than reflecting the world around them by rephrasing, describing, or summarizing; they are identifying how ideas or items are interconnected. Relationships between items or events are of a number of different types:

Comparison—indicating that two or more items or ideas share a common characteristic

Contrast—indicating that two or more ideas or items differ in a particular characteristic

Classification—indicating that an item or idea belongs to a previously defined category; statements of classification may be based on a comparison

Qualitative relationship—indicating which items or ideas occupy a higher or lower position in a hierarchy; for example, bigger, taller, more of

Sequential relationship—indicating the sequential order in which items, events, or ideas come; for example, first, second, third

Explanation—indicating reasons for something: telling what caused something to happen, explaining an event in terms of a general principle[10]

Some examples may clarify.

Comparing   The student identifies ways in which ideas or items are similar.

What the student does:	*What the student says:*
The student examines two flowers— a lily and a tulip.	"Both flowers have three petals."
The student considers several poems.	"None of these poems rhyme."
The student studies the maps of three countries.	"In all three countries, the land is mainly mountainous."

Contrasting   The student identifies ways in which ideas or items differ.

What the student does:	*What the student says:*
The student considers three plays.	"Play X is set in an urban apartment whereas Play Y has a different setting; it's on a remote island. Play Z? It's hard to tell just where it is set."
The student studies two wooden blocks.	"One block's red. The other one is green."
The student examines two flowers— a tulip and an apple blossom.	"The apple flower has five petals; the tulip is different. It has only three."

---

10. *Ibid.*, pp. 9-10.

Classification   The student looks at one or more items or ideas and puts them into a predefined group; basically he says, "these belong together."

What the student does:	*What the student says:*
The student studies a new sample of rock.	"This is igneous."
The student considers a poem he has not seen before.	"I think this poem belongs to the poet's early period."
The student picks out the improper fraction from among 2/3, 4/5, 7/3, 7/20, 1/2.	"7/3."

Qualitative analysis   The student basically is saying that one item or idea has more or less of a quality.

What the student does:	*What the student says:*
The student examines several samples of microorganisms under a microscope.	"Sample A is a more complex form of organism than is Sample B."
The student studies a map showing numbers of cities.	"City T is at a higher altitude than City H."
The student studies several sound samples.	"Sound X has a higher pitch than Sound Y."

Sequential analysis   The student basically is saying that this came first, that second, and so on.

What the student does:	*What the student says:*
The student studies a listing of events arranged nonsequentially.	"A happened first, B second, C last."

Explaining   The student explains what caused something to happen or he explains a particular event or sample in terms of an accepted principle or principles; he explains why by suggesting what human motivation triggered the event.

What the student does:	*What the student says:*
The student is asked why he connected certain pieces of equipment together.	"I did it to prevent the water from leaking all over the floor."
The student is asked why he categorized X play as a comedy.	"Because most comedies do not emphasize human suffering and failings; this play does not have a theme of human failing."

The student is asked to study the story to find out why Pippo went into the trailer.	"Because Pippo knew the parrot was in the trailer and he wanted to hear it talk."
The student is asked why the object kept moving even though the student stopped pushing it.	"Inertia—like Newton said, you gotta have another force to stop it."

Several thoughts have probably occurred to the reader of the previous listing of statements representing relational thinking. First, under different conditions, the statements made by students might well represent recall. The student who says, "This came first, then that," may be simply recalling if the teacher has already explained or if he has read that sequence. What is significant is the condition under which the student emits the statement—whether he is figuring out the relationship himself. To relate is to figure out or to put interconnected pieces together.

Second, the lines separating different varieties of relational thinking are far from clear-cut; one thinking process blurs into the next. After all, qualitative analysis is a form of contrasting; classifying requires some comparison. Although this poses a problem for scientific study of classroom interaction, the lack of clear-cut boundaries between categories is not that great a concern for the teacher. The teacher is more interested in obtaining a general notion of whether students are being involved in higher levels of thinking, not in collecting highly reliable data on interaction. The teacher's goal is to develop his own awareness of the general kinds of thinking represented by student statements.

Projecting

When students are faced with some problems, they must take a large cognitive leap and move from the given into the unknown. They do this when they predict what might happen, when they make inferences, when they use knowledge to design new ways of doing things or looking at knowledge, when they apply their knowledge to a new situation.

A few examples will clarify thinking that involves leaps beyond the observable:

What the student does:	*What the student says:*
The student is looking at the picture of a school bus in which one child is running to catch the bus; he predicts—	"That boy gonna miss the bus."

A student is beginning to heat solid sulfur; he hypothesizes—	"I think this stuff is either going to melt or burn when I get the temperature up there."
A student examines a listing of specific items on the board.	"We can classify what we've got there under two headings: Sounds of Nature and Sounds of Machines."
A student examines some data being collected.	"Let's record our data in this form" (and he gives his original design).
A student examines a sentence that needs to be punctuated.	"Put commas around the words *his sister*."
A student tries to spell *panicking*.	"Well, you add a *k* to *picnicking* so you must have to spell *panicking* with a *k*, too."

As shown by these examples, projecting involves students in predicting what will happen or saying how to handle new situations; the student basically is projecting: "Given all that I know, this is the way to do it or these are the things that will occur." Some projections may have very little basis in fact as in the prediction that the boy will miss the bus; other projections are hypotheses—scientific predictions based on previous encounters with similar phenomena. The fellow who hypothesizes that sulfur will either melt or burn is probably basing his prediction on his experiences with ice, lead, wood, and/or magnesium. What he does is apply understanding gleaned in other situations to a new but related situation.

Students also apply their understanding of rules and procedures to new situations. This is what a boy does when he punctuates a sentence not encountered before but which is similar to situations previously handled. Likewise, a girl projects when she tells how to solve a mathematics problem she has not solved before but that is similar to problems previously worked.

When students draw inferences from what people are saying to them, they are similarly bringing their past experiences into a new situation. A person who says: "I guess you are telling me you don't agree," when someone does not respond to a statement he has just made is inferring. In the past, the speaker has found that when some people do not agree, they do not say so explicitly; they just keep quiet. In the new situation, the speaker assumes that the listener is behaving as others have done before and infers disagreement.

Another form of projecting is designing new ways of handling operations, facts, or ideas. The person who sees that all the items

noted so far can be grouped under two original headings is designing a category system—be it a rather unsophisticated one. The
person who sees that a particular task can be carried out in a new
way is similarly involved with design. In designing, a person starts
with the known to develop something new.

Obviously, ability to project beyond what is given—to apply,
predict, hypothesize, infer, design—is based on ability to relate and
to recall. The hypothesizer must have workable knowledge of
similar phenomena and be able to relate the immediate situation to
similar occurrences, before he can make his leap into prediction.
As Benjamin Bloom concludes in *Taxonomy of Educational Objectives*, sophisticated thinking strategies include some elements of
less sophisticated strategies.[11]

Valuing

Student statements sometimes represent a personal evaluation;
they carry an element of grading, praise, blame, commendation, or
criticism.[12] Semantic clues signal a valuing statement, clues such as
"I prefer . . .," "That is good . . .," "Now, my opinion is . . .,"
"What I think we should do (or should have done) is . . . ."

Arno Bellack distinguishes between an evaluative statement
that simply states an opinion and one that supports the opinion
with reasons. Bellack defines opinion as the making of statements
in which the speaker gives an evaluation regarding "(a) what should
or ought to be done, or (b) fairness, worth, importance, or quality
of an action, event, person, idea, plan or policy." Justifying statements are those in which reasons are given for holding the opinion.[13] To Bellack, students are opining when they state:

> "I like the way Martin Luther King handled himself before an audience."
> "We should wash our hands before we eat snack."
> "War is bad."
> "Russia was wrong to move into Czechoslovakia."
> "It is important for America to stay strong."

They are justifying when they add:

> "They shouldn't have done that; no country has a right to tell another
> country what to do."

---

11. Bloom, *op. cit.*, p. 18.
12. Bellack, *op. cit.*, p. 25.
13. *Ibid.*, pp. 25-26.

"I like Langston Hughes' poems better than Wordsworth's. Hughes'
poems express what's going on today. They're with it."

"I think my paper was an A paper. I did everything you said—used
lots of references, considered causes not just facts."

Bellack's distinction is an important one for the teacher who wants
to help students go beyond superficial valuing. A teacher who recog-
nizes an opining statement can encourage the student to give reasons.
The teacher follows up with: "Why do you believe that?" or "Why
do you prefer that?"

Inventing

Another kind of thinking found in classrooms—especially elementary
classrooms—is inventing. Inventing statements signify that the student is working in the realm of imagination or fantasy. Here an
example will clarify more easily than an explanation. Children in a
first-grade class are experiencing a flight of the imagination. The
teacher begins a story: "Now Micky was crawling through the dense
woods. All of a sudden . . ." The teacher gestures to a child with
whom she has made eye contact, and the child continues the story
line; the child invents: "Micky saw a big, big orange fire thing,
and it burnt his eyes something awful." Another child adds: "Micky
hid in the bushes." And another child invents: "I was so scared I
ran and ran!" And still another child: "The big fire ball was following
me. . . . It turned into a goblin."

Youngsters in this class are story-inventing in an oral-writing
experience. Their statements make no attempt to explain logically,
although some elements of explanation may be present. Their
statements do not describe realistically, although there is some
attempt at imaginative description. They are putting ideas together
and coming up with something that never happened exactly as they
invent it.

In oral-poetry-writing sessions and in brainstorming sessions,
students also think in inventive patterns. For instance, youngsters
begin with a word such as *slippery*. One youngster tosses out a line
such as:

Slippery, slippery slide

Another youngster takes up the invention and adds:

Makes me feel all funny inside

Another continues:

Takes me for a sliding ride

And another tries to end with:

> That's why I like the slippery slide

only to be climaxed by another who shouts out:

> Eeeeeeeekkkkkkkkk!

These youngsters are thinking with inventive twists. They are putting words together in imaginative patterns based on sound and feel rather than on logic.

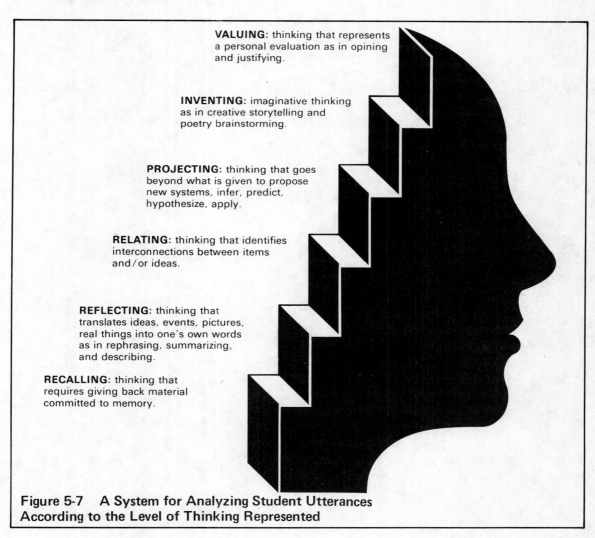

VALUING: thinking that represents a personal evaluation as in opining and justifying.

INVENTING: imaginative thinking as in creative storytelling and poetry brainstorming.

PROJECTING: thinking that goes beyond what is given to propose new systems, infer, predict, hypothesize, apply.

RELATING: thinking that identifies interconnections between items and/or ideas.

REFLECTING: thinking that translates ideas, events, pictures, real things into one's own words as in rephrasing, summarizing, and describing.

RECALLING: thinking that requires giving back material committed to memory.

Figure 5-7   A System for Analyzing Student Utterances According to the Level of Thinking Represented

Activities for Analyzing Student Statements

1. An easy way to begin to analyze the thought levels represented by student talk is to use two categories: recall and more-than-recall. More-than-recall includes reflecting, projecting, relating, inventing, valuing. Listen to a tape or to a live session of classroom discussion. Categorize each student contributing statement as either *recall* or *more-than-recall*, and tally the statement. Remember to consider each statement in context; a statement of a rule or generalization represents recall if the student is repeating something read or heard.

	Tallies	Number of Tallies
Recall		
More-than-recall		
Total Number of Tallies Recorded		

Determine the percentage of student statements representing recall by the formula:

$$\frac{\text{Number of statements representing recall}}{\text{Total number of statements tallied}} \times 100 = \text{percentage of student statements representing recall}$$

2. Make a value judgment after having analyzed the percentage of recall represented by student utterances in a particular class. Is the percentage excessive? too low? Support your opinion with a reason.

3. As you listen to classroom interaction, find examples of student utterances that represent rephrasing, summarizing, and/or describing. Write down what the student was doing as well as what the student said. Discuss your examples with another teacher or teacher-intern to see if others agree with the way you have categorized your examples.

4. On another occasion, see if you can identify student utterances that indicate that students are relating ideas or items through comparing, contrasting, classifying, analyzing, explaining. Again record examples noting both what the student was doing and what he was saying; discuss your examples with other teachers-in-training to see if you agree on what comprises relational thinking.

5. On still another occasion focus on valuing statements, recording examples. In your observations, do you find more valuing statements that could be considered examples of justifying? opining?

6. Study classroom interaction focusing on statements representing projecting. Look for statements that predict, hypothesize, or infer. Are there statements that suggest that students are involved in designing their own systems or applying generalizations in new situations? If so, record examples to discuss with other teachers.

7. In carrying out activities 3 to 6, you may have had difficulty finding examples from actual classroom interaction. Which kinds of thinking did you find nonexistent or limited in the discussion sessions you studied? Compare your data with other analyzers to determine whether there are some kinds of thinking that occur rarely in classrooms.

8. As you teach, look for examples of student statements that represent thinking above the level of recall. You may find this easier to do if—during a session—you focus on one kind of thinking, and record examples at the end of the lesson. Again share your examples with other teachers or teachers-in-training and identify kinds of thinking that occur on a limited basis in your class.

INTERPRETING IMPLIED MEANINGS

Although many investigators of verbal classroom interaction have studied the cognitive components of interaction, comparatively few have focused on implied meanings. The probable reason for this lack of stress is that emotional undertones are relatively difficult to investigate with any degree of reliability. However, the teacher who is using interaction analysis to gain additional competency in communicating with students can gain from informal study of meanings expressed implicitly rather than explicitly. The work of the semanticists is helpful in this case.

In *Language in Thought and Action*, S. I. Hayakawa comments on the favorable or unfavorable feelings that words can communicate. Hayakawa shows this by comparing two descriptions of the same man:

1. "He had apparently not shaved for several days, and his face and hands were covered with grime. His shoes were torn, and his coat, which was several sizes too small for him, was spotted with dried clay."
2. "Although his face was bearded and neglected, his eyes were clear and he looked straight ahead as he walked rapidly down the road. He seemed very tall; perhaps the fact that his coat was too small for him emphasized that impression. He was carrying a book under his left arm, and a small terrier ran at his heels."[14]

In neither description is a judgment explicitly stated, but the choice of details or the subordination of unfavorable details communicates the speaker's slant or point of view. One speaker is positively attuned to the man-of-the-road; the other has a negative view.

The words chosen to represent those details can similarly imply a judgment. Is he a man-of-the-road? a hobo? a derelict? The label assigned expresses the speaker's opinion of the man.

---

14. From *Language in Thought and Action*, Second Edition by S. I. Hayakawa, p. 47; copyright, 1941, 1949, © 1963, 1964 by Harcourt Brace Jovanovich, Inc. and reprinted with their permission and permission of George Allen & Unwin, Ltd.

Hayakawa offers the concept of snarl-words and purr-words to emphasize the idea that words can carry an implied judgment. Included within a larger utterance, purr-words suggest: "I like," or "This is superior." Snarl-words suggest: "I don't like," "This is inferior," or even "I hate."[15]

Snarl-words and purr-words are oftentimes tucked into statements of description, summary, or relationships and thus their emotional meanings can be easily overlooked. But as Hayakawa comments, it is important to allocate meanings correctly—to perceive the judgmental quality of the communication and to realize that the words selected are more an indication of the speaker's point of view than they are a reflection of what is.[16]

Snarl-words appear in a variety of contexts. Negative labels have been and are used to refer to national, religious, and racial groups; they therefore can give an indication of the prejudices harbored by a speaker. Youngsters dream up snarl names to hurl at other youngsters they dislike or to refer to the teacher behind his back. A disliked teacher may secretly be called: "The Little Dictator," "Hitler," "The Queen Bee"; peers may be referred to more openly as "The Ant," "Rodent," "Pest," "Whale."

Purr-words are part of the language of persuasion, of flattery, and of social propriety. Advertisements make plentiful use of purr-words as the ad men tell us to eat the "breakfast of champions" (implied message: you can become a champion) or to join the Pepsi generation (implied message: the Pepsi generation is youthful). Flattery, too, relies upon purr-words; the saleslady tells the stout matron that she isn't fat—she is pleasingly plump. Sometimes in everyday jargon, we say of people who go overboard with purr-words, "He really laid it on thick." Then, too, purr-words have been coined to overcome unpleasant feelings or negative connotations associated with the original terms; the purr-word is the socially accepted way of referring to things or people. The purr-word in the following pairs is obvious:

Garbage man	Sanitation man
Undertaker	Mortician
Janitor	Custodian

The problem inherent in any interpretation of purr-words and

---

15. *Ibid.*, pp. 44-45.
16. *Ibid.*, p. 45.

snarl-words is that words themselves have no meaning. As William Brooks points out in his book *Speech Communication*, words are only symbols for things; it is people who attach meanings to the word symbols. Meanings are "in people."[17] Study, for example, the underlined words in the following list and indicate the category to which each belongs: P for purr-words, S for snarl-words, and N for neutral words that carry no implied positive or negative judgment to you:

_____   He is a square.

_____   He is a hard hat.

_____   She is a political candidate.

_____   He is a militant.

_____   She is a liberated woman.

_____   That man is a Communist.

Probably no two people in a group will categorize all the words in an identical way. Brooks gives the example of a sixteen-year-old youth who remarked to his grandfather that a television entertainer they were watching was square. The grandfather concurred, adding, "Yes, the entertainer was honest." The older man was using the meaning of *square* associated with *square dealer* and *square shooter*— which shows that the meanings people assign to word symbols change and can be a factor in the generation gap.[18]

When the teacher attempts to listen to the implied meanings contained in a student utterance, the teacher must go beyond his own perception of the meanings attached to word symbols to consider what meanings the word holds for the student. William Brooks writes that to do this the listener must (1) be highly aware of the ambiguity of language, realizing that words mean many things, that what is a purr-word to one person may be a snarl-word to a second person; (2) be conscious that meanings attached to words are derived from past experiences; and (3) be conscious of projecting his own meanings onto what others say.[19] The subjectivity of such

17. William Brooks, *Speech Communication* (Dubuque, Iowa: Wm. C. Brown Co., 1971), pp. 37-38.
18. *Ibid.*, p. 38.
19. *Ibid.*, p. 40.

interpretation shows again why the systematic investigators of classroom interaction have left such considerations to the semanticists.

Tone of voice, pitch, and loudness of projection are clues to be used in interpreting implied meanings. The work of Joel Davitz referred to earlier suggests that people do express feelings vocally and that these feelings can be perceived by others. Davitz concludes that the vocal aspects of speech may reflect "the level of activation associated with particular emotional states"; in other words, feelings that are active—for example, hate, anger, fear, love—are reflected in the voice.[20] Rising pitch, heightened intensity of speech, harsh tone can suggest that words have high emotional significance to a speaker and are indeed snarl-words to him. The investigators of body language would add facial expressions, gestures, stance as clues to implied meanings.

Activities for Interpreting Implied Meanings

1. Listen to the words used by students as they report or describe. Identify words and phrases that are loaded with implied meaning. You can do this systematically as you watch a class you are not teaching or a class you are viewing on videotape replay. Record examples for discussion with other teachers or teacher-interns:

Words Spoken	Implied Meaning	Clues That Suggested the Student Was Implying More Than He Said

2. As you teach a discussion session, concentrate on possible implied meanings that indicate how students feel about the

---

20. Joel Davitz, *The Communication of Emotional Meaning* (New York: McGraw-Hill, 1964), p. 195.

topic under discussion. Use the feedback you pick up in this way to help students talk about their feelings.

3. Read Chapter 6 of Hayakawa's *Language in Thought and Action;* there you will find a thorough explanation of connotative language.

ACCEPTING DIFFERENCES

When you speak, do you tend to say, "He be playin' every morning," or do you say, "He plays every morning"? Do you say, "She a good cat," or "She is a good cat"? Do you say, "Leroy work at night," or "Leroy works at night"? Do you say, "I asks did he want twenty cent," or "I asked if he wanted twenty cents"? Do you select "I ain't go," rather than "I didn't go"?

Anyone who has grown up speaking a variety of standard English will probably have responded with the second option of either pair and may consider the option he has chosen as more acceptable than the other. However, present-day linguists agree that neither option is inherently superior as a means of communication. Their research indicates that the first option of each pair is part of a "well-ordered, highly structured, highly developed language system which in many aspects is different from standard English."[21] The linguists term the language system, of which each of the first options is a sample, *black nonstandard English.*

In the past ten years, two positions regarding the nature of nonstandard dialects of English have been stated—the position of the linguists often referred to as a *difference model* and a second position referred to as a *deficit model.*[22] Since teachers' attitudes toward nonstandard dialects may well determine the way they approach communication with students who speak a dialect such as black nonstandard, let us consider the distinction between the two positions.

A basic premise of those who espouse a deficit theory is that the nonstandard dialect is an inferior vehicle for communicating, lacking in both vocabulary and structural patterns to express thoughts, especially complex thoughts. According to this thesis, nonstandard dialects are restrictive; they limit the ability of speakers to perform logical thinking operations.

21. Joan C. Baratz, "Language and Cognitive Assessment of Negro Children: Assumptions and Research Needs," *American Speech and Hearing Association,* vol. 11, no. 3, 1969, p. 88.
22. Joan C. Baratz, "A Bi-Dialectal Task for Determining Language Proficiency in Economically Disadvantaged Negro Children," Eric Document No. 020 519, 1968.

Many theorists who have developed this point of view base
their conclusions on research in which black children who speak
a variety of nonstandard English are asked to react to or produce
sound patterns and/or syntactic structures that characterize
standard English. For instance, Cynthia Deutsch investigated
auditory discrimination of lower-class black children.[23] Using the
Wepman Auditory Discrimination Test, Ms. Deutsh asked the children to distinguish between word pairs such as *wreath* and *reef*.
Walt Wolfram points out, however, that in black nonstandard
dialect *th* is consistently pronounced *f* when the *th* appears at the
end of a word. The inability of black children to make the distinction between *reef* and *wreath* on the Wepman Test relates to the
different sound systems of their language, rather than to a defi-
ciency.[24]

Proponents of a deficit theory go on to relate cognitive
functioning to differences in the way sentences are constructed in
nonstandard English. According to this line of thought, to carry
out the kind of thinking necessary to describe, one must be able
to think and say, "The ball is red; it is not blue."[25] Because in
black nonstandard English, the sentence would be stated, "The
ball red," the deficit model contends that the "lack" of the
appropriate language pattern prevents a speaker from fully carrying out the thinking strategy—in this case, description. As Wolfram
and others have pointed out, however, many languages—Russian
and Hungarian, for example—delete the linking verb (the copula)
in this construction. Few would contend that the language patterns
of the Russians or Hungarians interfere with their ability to perform the related logical process. In contrast, the research of the
linguists seems to demonstrate that "any logical operation possible
in a standard dialect is also possible in a nonstandard dialect."[26]

Scope of vocabulary has also been investigated by those adher-
ing to a deficit model. Because speakers of black nonstandard
English tend to score lower than speakers of standard English on
standardized vocabulary tests, it has been suggested that the nonstandard dialect offers the nonstandard speaker a limited word

23. Cynthia Deutsch, "Auditory Discrimination and Learning: Social Factors," *Merrill-Palmer Quarterly*, vol. 10, no. 1, 1964, pp. 277-296.

24. Walt Wolfram, "The Nature of Nonstandard Dialect Divergence," *Elementary English*, vol. 47, no. 5, May 1970, pp. 739-748.

25. C. Bereiter, and S. Engelmann, *Teaching Disadvantaged Children in Preschool* (Engle-wood Cliffs, N.J.: Prentice-Hall, 1966).

26. Wolfram, *op. cit.*

pool from which to draw. William Labov's studies in the black English venacular reported in *Language in the Inner City* indicate just the opposite. Utterances made by members of street gangs are evidence that speakers of nonstandard dialects do not lack in words to express their thoughts.[27] Some words used are unique to the dialect, and at times words in standard English are given a different meaning. For example, in black idiom, *rapping, jiving, sounding, shucking, gripping*, and *signifying* are all words used to distinguish different forms of talking.[28] Yet the speaker of standard English would be hard put to define these terms as explicitly as did the members of the Chicago street gang from whom Thomas Kochman got his definitions. The example makes clear the problem of studying the breadth of vocabulary of nonstandard speakers. Most tests used in the past and present measure understanding of words in standard dialect and make no attempt to measure the actual word pool of speakers who employ a less common dialect. How many standardized vocabulary tests, for instance, include items such as *shucking, sounding*, and *gripping*?

To explain the supposed lack of vocabulary and limited structural patterns in nonstandard dialects, proponents of the deficit theory have turned to a cultural argument. They suggest that: "The speech heard at home is meager with little elaboration"; or "The mother is preoccupied with survival and, therefore, makes little verbal contact with her children"; or "The home environment is noisy and crowded leading to limited auditory discrimination"; or even "Verbal ability is not respected in the ghetto."

The linguists are horrified by such explanations. They draw upon syntactic analysis of dialects to show that nonstandard dialects exhibit highly predictable and consistent sentence patterns. One of the most comprehensive discussions of the syntactic patterns of black nonstandard English is found in J. L. Dillard's *Black English*. Dillard describes extensively the syntactic characteristics of black English; some of the structural characteristics he identifies include:

> In black English, no final *-s* is added to the third person singular verb as in *he go, he love, John run*.

27. William Labov, *Language in the Inner City* (Philadelphia: University of Pennsylvania Press, 1972).
28. Thomas Kochman, "Rapping in the Ghetto," *TRANS-action*, vol. 6, no. 4, 1969, pp. 26-34.

Ain' is used as a negative marker as in *He ain' go* to refer to momentary action generally in the past or in *He ain' goin'* to refer to progressive action generally in the present.

Be is used to express continuous or "stretched out" action as in *He be waitin' for me every night.*

Is serves the auxiliary function filled by *have* in standard English as in *Is they gone there?* or *The men is all died.*

The copula or linking verb is eliminated in constructions such as *the box blue; he a sly cat.*

Plural nouns do not require an *-s* ending when numerals modify the noun as in *a million dollar, twenty cent.*

Here go is used much in the style of the French *voici* and *voila* to mean "here is" or "there is" as in the sentence *Here go a table.*

Possession is shown by juxtaposition as in *Mary hat* or *he book.*[29]

As Joan Baratz points out, ability to reproduce and to put together sentences in the complex patterns of black nonstandard dialect comes through constant exposure to the syntatic patterns of the language. Just as the speaker of Castilian Spanish learns the syntax of his language through exposure to it in childhood so black children learn "language in the context of their environment."[30] Based on her research, Baratz contends also that when speakers of a dialect known from childhood attempt to use a different dialect, there is interference from the "native" dialect. This interference affects both the speaker of standard English when asked to repeat utterances from black nonstandard English and speakers of nonstandard English when asked to repeat utterances from standard English.[31] The difficulty in repeating the utterances stems from differences between the two systems, not in carelessness, lack of auditory discrimination, or lack of related cognitive abilities.

The ideas being developed by the linguists reveal a number of implications for teachers who are concerned with the interactive patterns in classrooms. Understanding of dialectal differences will doubtless influence the way teachers approach the speech of those using nonstandard dialects. If teachers adhere to the deficit position, they may react to students' vocabulary, syntax, or pronunciation rather than to the substance of the communication. Teachers may

---

29. J. L. Dillard, *Black English* (New York: Random House, 1972), chap. 2.
30. Baratz, 1969, *op. cit.*, p. 89.
31. *Ibid.*, p. 90.

stop the student to correct—correct meaning to translate the student's communication into standard English. In so doing, teachers may imply that the students' first dialect is deficient and may undermine students' respect for themselves and their culture. Students may react by not bothering to contribute in a language system that meets with constant rejection.

In contrast, teachers who adhere to a difference position accept the students' dialect as a system having communication power; as a result, they are less likely to interject correcting remarks that imply the dialect is inferior. They realize that "the children are being careful, consistent, and graceful within the only dialect they know,"[32] and encourage children to express themselves. Of course, they may believe with some linguists that it is useful for students, who live in a society in which a variety of standard English is the prestige dialect, to add the prestige dialect to their language repertoire. Taking this position, they may integrate activities into the curriculum that will help students become biloquial—able to handle both dialects depending on what the social situation demands.

Activities to Study Dialectal Differences

1. Study a tape of classroom interaction in which a teacher is talking with students who speak a nonstandard dialect. From what you observe, do you think that the teacher adheres to a deficit or a difference model?
2. If you teach students who speak a nonstandard dialect of English, listen to a tape recording of a discussion session. Consider your own reactions to nonstandard syntax, punctuation, and vocabulary.
3. Summarize the key points of the linguists' argument supporting a difference interpretation of nonstandard dialects. Then express your own point of view on the issue.
4. Read Chapter 2 and Chapter 7 of J. L. Dillard's *Black English*, (New York: Random House, 1972.)

---

32. Roger Shuy, "Detroit Speech: Careless, Awkward, and Inconsistent, or Systematic, Graceful, and Regular?" *Elementary English*, vol. 45, no. 5, May 1968, pp. 565-569.

THE TEACHER AS SOURCE-ENCODER

To a large extent teachers determine the amount and kind of student talk, the levels of thinking represented by student statements, the kinds of participatory motions emitted by students. One way teachers control the nature of students verbal and nonverbal utterances is through their own verbal and nonverbal statements. The questions teachers ask and the sequence in which they ask the questions are determinants of the resulting levels of thinking represented by student talk. Gestures, eye movements and facial expressions help to focus and restore attention. Even the speed of motion and talk can communicate urgency or lack of concern and can cause students to vary the speed of their activity.

Because of the relationship between student and teacher utterances, the kinds of analyses carried out in Focus Two lay the foundation for analyses of teacher statements that will be described in Focus Three. Teachers who discover that the amount and kind of student statements emitted in their classrooms do not meet their own standards of acceptability can analyze aspects of their verbal and nonverbal utterances to see if they can discover ways of varying communication patterns.

Module 6 has been designed to give the teacher insight into the complexities of teaching strategies that are primarily verbal; through the module, the teacher begins to develop competencies in verbal encoding. Module 7 has been designed to help the teacher become more effective in encoding nonverbal messages. Module 8 continues in the direction set in Module 7 by considering the nonverbal variables of space and time.

MODULE GOALS

The teacher gains competency in—

communicating within various interaction formats

using the form of solicitation that relates most directly to
    goals sought

varying his reacting moves to meet the needs of the situation

building student responses and questions into his reactions

structuring and responding so students understand where
    they are going

planning interactive sequences and asking questions that
    guide students from the less to the more abstract

designing verbal materials for small groups and individuals
    that are sequenced so that students begin by gathering
    information and move to processing information and
    abstracting

designing sequences in which students raise key questions

varying wait-time dependent on the kind of thinking being
    solicited

handling diverse sentence patterns

MODULE 6
Sending Verbal
Messages

Mr. Larchmont's class settled into their seats as Larchmont walked to the front, picked up his roll book, and remarked: "Let's check attendance." He called the roll, each student responding with a fast "Here." Then Larchmont put down his book, held up a long-handled, thick-bristled paintbrush, closed the distance between himself and the group, and began: "Today we're going to try our hand at painting without diluting our tempera and with a dry brush on which we have mixed our paints directly. Some people call the technique the Japanese brush stroke. The results are rather different from that produced with water colors. Let me show you. I'm going to rotate one side of this brush into the green tempera paint that I've poured into our paint cups; then I'll rotate the other side of the brush into the white paint—just a little bit, not too much so I don't dilute my green too much. OK. Now. Using the tip of my brush, I'm going to sketch stems and leaves onto a black background. Notice how I hold my brush. Be careful not to flatten the brush too much; your lines get too fat. All right, now let's say that I want to paint some pink blossoms on the stems. I'll get a clean brush. And how will I mix my paint?"

A student made a joining motion. Larchmont recognized the motion with a nod of his head, and the student answered, "You dip one side of the brush in the red and the other side in the white."

"Does it have to be just white?" Larchmont countered.

"I guess not; I guess you could dip a little bit of the brush in maybe yellow to get a different effect," was her reply.

112

Mr. Larchmont followed her directions, then quickly outlined a flower on his demonstration sheet. "Anyone want to make a fast try?" Several students indicated willingness. Larchmont chose: "Eric!" and Eric came forward to demonstrate. His flower was not that great; the class snickered its reaction. Larchmont interjected, "Not bad for a first try. Your first try might not set the world on fire either." Then he added, "Remember, you don't have to all draw flowers. All I need is thirty-two flower pictures! You can do anything you want—leaves swirling, trees bending, fire burning—but the technique seems to work best on nature themes. Any questions?" The students shook their heads. He responded with an "OK. Get to work!"

The students got out their materials and soon were engrossed in the activity. Larchmont circulated, giving individual help and encouragement. His comments made to individual students were almost continuous: "Rotate your brush a bit more when you dip it in the paint." "Have you planned where your painting is going?" "Do you think it needs more white?" Once in a while he addressed the entire class: "Keep your voices down." "We have only fifteen minutes left." "Some of your stuff is good." And finally, "That's it. We've gotta clean up. Hang your paintings on the clothespins. Consolidate the paint you've used. All red here, green there, and so forth." And in the last moment, "We'll do this again next time. Think about a subject to work with."

As this episode shows, sending verbal messages is an integral part of teaching not only in a traditional teacher-led discussion but also in an individualized laboratory-type experience. The teacher uses words under a variety of conditions to achieve a variety of pedagogical purposes—to direct, question, answer, explain, encourage—even to tease a bit. In so doing, he sets the limits within which learning takes place. What he says determines to a large extent what students do and how they do it, what students think and how they think it, what feelings students take away with them. Because teacher talk is such a pivotal factor in classroom interaction, high-level skill in using talk effectively and efficiently is essential for the teacher. It is in this context that analysis of verbal interaction has much to offer.

IDENTIFYING TALK FORMATS

Analysis of teacher talk can begin rather simply with consideration of the context in which communication is occurring. Mr. Larchmont allocated most of his class time to a one-teacher/individual-student format. He circulated from student to student talking not to masses of students at one time but on a one-to-one basis. Generally, the one-teacher/individual-student talk format is reserved by the teacher for helping students working on studies or projects at their own rates, for spotting individual problems, for remedying those problems, and for counseling. It is the format found very often in open classrooms.

A second format is the one-teacher/subclass model. Here the teacher breaks the class into subclasses or groups that are smaller in size than the total class, and speaks to one subclass. In shifting from a one-teacher/individual-student format to a one-teacher/

Figure 6-1   Talk Formats

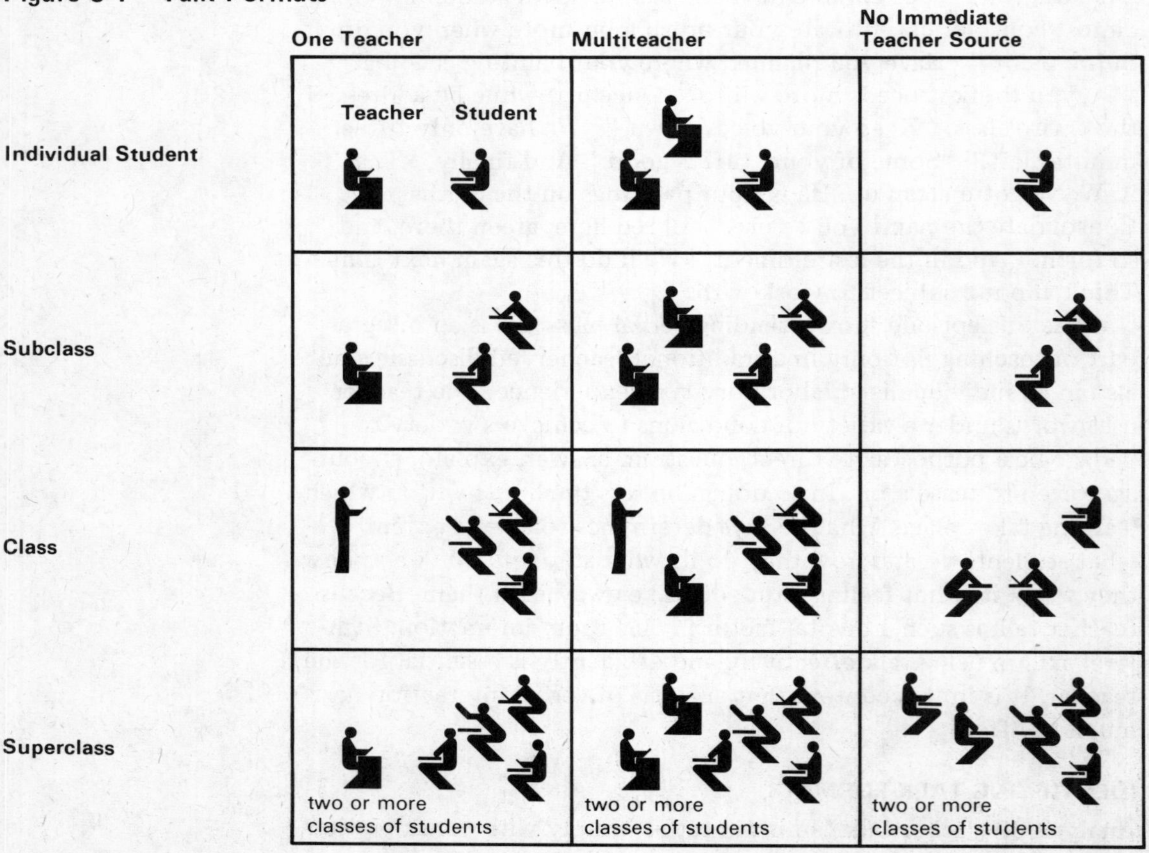

subclass format, the teacher increases the number of students with whom he interacts at one time; in so doing he may increase the range of ideas contributed but may limit the input from any one participant and the emphasis placed on the unique needs of individuals. Teachers typically use the one-teacher/subclass format for working with students who have common needs and/or interests and for stimulating small-group project activity. Reading in elementary grades is very often taught within this communication format.

Perhaps the most frequently encountered format is one-teacher/total-class. Larchmont selected this format for giving directions needed by all students, for handling managerial tasks such as attendance taking, for introducing the topic of the lesson. It is a format many teachers use for carrying on general discussions and for presenting material as in a lecture. The format limits needless repetition of information; all students receive information at the same time in the same dose. In addition, it increases the range of ideas as numbers of differing opinions may be offered. Conversely, the format increases the diversity of the participants; when this diversity is in interest or ability, individual learning problems may be lost in the crowd. It limits the number of direct contributions by each participant.

A far less frequently encountered format for verbal interaction is one-teacher/superclass. Such a format occurs when one teacher assumes leadership responsibility for two or more classes of students and conducts the superclass as a whole, leading them in discussion, giving directions, announcing, preparing them for a film or speaker. One-teacher/superclass sessions occur generally in assembly-type settings or situations in which a teaching team is cooperatively responsible for the learning of several classes of students, and one teacher conducts the entire group.

The four formats described so far bring one teacher into interaction with one or more students. Conceivably, in team-teaching situations, classroom interaction that involves more than one teacher simultaneously with one or more students can occur. Two or more teachers can communicate with one youngster studying individually; the result is a multiteacher/individual-student format that resembles a consultation. Two or more teachers can work with a small group of students, each making a contribution to the discussion; the result is a multiteacher/subclass format. Two or more teachers can lead a class of students, with each of the teachers interjecting verbal utterances, the result being a multiteacher/total-class format. And several teachers can lead a superclass, each teacher making a verbal contribution to the multiteacher/superclass interaction. Even brief periods spent in classroom observation indicate little use of such diverse formats. Teachers tend to communicate in a one-teacher/individual-student, subclass, or total-class format.

Another series of formats appears when the teacher withdraws from verbal interaction, leaving students to pursue study activities individually in what could be termed a no-immediate-teacher-source/individual-student format. Such would be the case when students "plug themselves into" listening stations, pursue reading or writing activity, work at library research, take a test. During this period of pursuit, the teacher makes no verbal contact with the student.

A no-immediate-teacher-source/subclass format is one in which a teacher divorces himself from subclass activity. This occurs in classrooms when work groups get to the point where the group is self-directed and knows how to handle its task. Again, the teacher makes no verbal contact; he literally "takes a back seat."

A related format—no-immediate-teacher-source/total-class—is found when students report, present panels, take over discussion leadership, and the teacher becomes a silent observer who interjects no verbal comments. The students run the class. If the group is comprised of more than one class, the format could be termed no-immediate-teacher-source/superclass. Such a situation occurs so infrequently that it is practically nonexistent.

Because typically a teacher selects an interaction format and maintains that format for substantial periods with only brief shifts to another pattern, the teacher in retrospect can rather easily describe the general patterns that emerge during a class hour. Larchmont, for instance, could describe his interaction as being one-teacher/total-class during the introductory portion of the hour. Then he shifted to one-teacher/individual-student and continued in this format for the remainder of the time with momentary reversions to the total class interaction to give general reminders and previews of things to come. Most of the time he was communicating one-to-one.

Another teacher might find his own pattern to be rather different. He might open with a one-teacher/total-class format that is maintained throughout the hour with a short break or two in which no-immediate-teacher-source/individual-student activity occurs when students read an assigned portion of their book.

Of course, this analysis results only in descriptions of the formats employed; teachers themselves must judge whether the format pattern chosen is meeting stated objectives.

Activities to Study Teacher-Talk Formats

1. After you have taught a lesson, outline the sequence of interaction formats in which you participated; approximate the time you spent in each format. You may end with data resembling the following:

First few minutes	One-teacher/individual-student
Next ten minutes	One-teacher/total-class
Next fifteen minutes	No-immediate-teacher-source/individual-student
Last twenty minutes	One-teacher/total-class

   In analyzing talk formats, focus on which interaction you as *teacher* are involved in. If you are talking with an individual student while other students are working in subgroups, the interaction is classed as one-teacher/individual-student.

2. Carry out activity 1 for four or five sessions. Generalize based on your listings of formats employed. Do you tend to restrict yourself to a single format? If so, which one? Are there some formats you never use? If so, which ones?

3. Design several activities to use with your students in which you select a talk format you use infrequently. For instance, if you tend to restrict yourself to one teacher/total-class, plan a session in which you employ one-teacher/subclass. Try out your plan and evaluate the results.

4. Join with another teacher or teacher-intern to lead a student discussion in the multiteacher/subclass, class, or superclass format. After, list what you consider to be the strengths and weaknesses of the format.

5. If you are not teaching, analyze the talk-format sequence in a class in which you are observing. Use a two-way recording chart, such as the one shown in Figure 6-1, tallying in each box. In order to record the sequence of the formats used and the time duration of each format, mark a tally at each sixty-second interval; when a teacher shifts to a different format

connect the last tally recorded in the box representing the previous format to the first tally in the box representing the new format.

ANALYZING PEDAGOGICAL MOVES

A teacher's verbal utterances—whether directed to an individual student, a subclass, a class, or a superclass—serve a pedagogical function; that is, utterances communicate different kinds of instructional messages.

One of the most potentially useful constructs for studying the pedagogical implications of a teacher's verbal statements is an analytical system devised by Arno Bellack and his associates. Bellack views classroom discourse as a language game, following Wittgenstein's theoretical model.[1] By and large, games have players, moves, and rules that explain what moves which players can make. In the classroom game, according to Bellack, the players are teachers and students; the moves are verbal ways in which the players communicate with one another.

As Bellack conceives the classroom language game, there are four major pedagogical moves: structuring, soliciting, responding, and reacting. The first two—structuring and soliciting—are initiatory: the player is launching, halting, directing, asking, telling. The latter two—responding and reacting—are reflexive: the player is answering, rating, modifying, concurring, disagreeing.[2] Let us consider each type of move to see how the teacher plays it in the "classroom game."

Structuring

Mr. Fitz verbally opened his class with a structuring move: "Today, boys and girls, we are going to begin a study of myths. Myths were written generally some time in the past by ancient people who were attempting to explain phenomena they did not really understand and often—ah—oftentimes—even feared. The myth we are going to start is one you may already know, 'Midas and the Golden Touch.' You may have heard about Midas muffler—something you might think about is why the Midas people chose that name. Well, anyway, we'll be reading and talking about a number of myths— later in the week—ah—ah—Tuesday—Pandora's box. . . ."

1. Arno Bellack, et al., *The Language of the Classroom* (New York: Teachers College Press, 1966), p. 13. Copyright 1966 by Teachers College Press; described by permission of the publisher.
2. *Ibid.*, pp. 4-5.

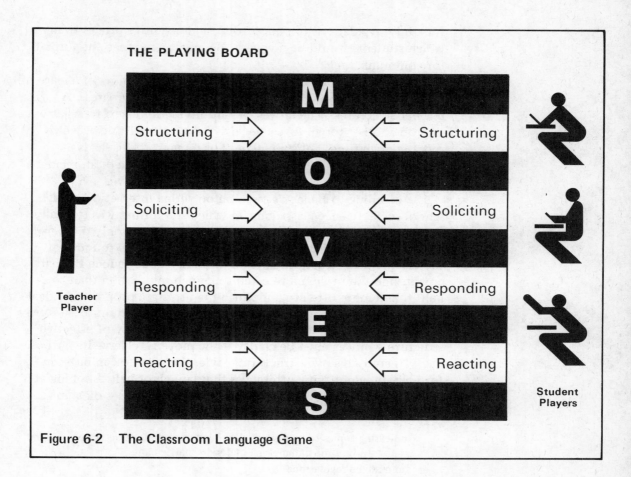

Figure 6-2   The Classroom Language Game

What was this teacher doing verbally? Bellack would say that the teacher was setting the stage for or launching interaction by announcing the topic of discussion (the myth), the agents who would be involved (the total class), the action to be taken (reading, talking, thinking about), the time span (today and into the week).[3] Through his structuring move, Fitz was mapping the boundaries in which students and teacher would operate. Additionally, Fitz was stating propositions about the subject matter being considered.

Structuring moves that launch interaction may include information about other dimensions of the activity. Fitz might go on to announce the instructional aid or aids to be used, the reasons

---

3. *Ibid.*, pp. 16-17.

for study, regulations to be followed, and cognitive processes in which students would be involved. He might announce the format for communicating.[4]

Structuring moves occur not only at the beginning of a learning encounter but also within an encounter already in progress. A teacher structures as he moves to halt interaction or to focus attention on another topic. A teacher may say: "All right now, we've spent enough time. Let's move on," or remark: "This leads us right into another point," or add: "That reminds me of an incident." In each case, the teacher is making a structuring move.

According to Bellack's research on verbal interaction in high school social science classrooms in which the format was typically one-teacher/total-class, structuring moves represent only 5.5 percent of all pedagogical moves identified. Bellack also found that the teacher uses structuring moves primarily to announce the participants and the topic, more often to launch interaction than to halt it, and more often to announce than to state propositions dealing with the subject matter to be considered.[5] Based on these functions of structuring, it appears that a primary quality of effective structuring moves must be clarity if the move is to serve its purpose.

To study his own structuring style, the teacher can begin informally by identifying utterances that launch or halt. Looking at recorded episodes of classroom interaction, he focuses on statements in which he is

indicating topics to be discussed, procedures, kinds of activities, reasons for study, time parameters, materials, participants

announcing regulations

changing to a new topic, procedure, activity

halting the total interaction or a phase of the interaction

Having gained a general notion of structuring, the teacher can consider his typical structuring behavior. Are there specific words repeated as he structures? Are there certain words repeated at key junctures? Sometimes a teacher intentionally repeats a series of words as he encounters students from day to day; students—hearing the key words—know what will happen, and their knowing simplifies classroom management. For instance, Larchmont typically told his students he was beginning by moving to the front of the room and

4. Bellack, *The Language of the Classroom*, pp. 134-135.
5. *Ibid.*, pp. 163-164.

announcing, "Let's check attendance." This was part of his *modus operandi.*

On the other hand, a teacher may not be conscious of his repetitive use of words. Probably, Mr. Larchmont was unaware of his continued use of *now* and *OK* as well as *all right, then,* and *be careful,* on which he relied heavily to make thought transitions. Used excessively, such words may annoy listeners.

A teacher's structuring repertoire also consists of sentence patterns that typify verbal activity. One teacher may use short, staccato sentences to structure; another may tend toward longer, more circuitous sentences; still another may vary sentences to meet the situation. Similarly, one teacher may tend toward imperatives, another toward parenthetical asides, and another toward a specific way of phrasing such as *Let me show you, Let me begin by, Let me explain.*

A third aspect of a teacher's structuring repertoire, which is open to analysis, is his overall approach. Some teachers like to launch with a short story related to the topic of the up-coming session; those with a sense of humor may open with jokes or lengthy anecdotes. Others launch and even halt without a lot of preliminaries. They launch by jumping, not working, into the subject. They halt with a simple statement of fact: "Time's up." Mr. Larchmont is a "jumper"; all business—he turns directly to the materials and procedures basic to the operation, and he halts with a succinct, "That's it!" Fitz probably falls into the jumping category as well.

Soliciting

A second kind of pedagogical move identified by Bellack is soliciting, a move used by teachers in Bellack's sample more frequently than any of the other three moves. Soliciting moves are utterances that ask for

a. "an active verbal response on the part of the persons addressed";
b. "a cognitive response, e.g., encouraging persons addressed to attend to something"; or
c. "a physical response."[6]

According to Bellack's definition, Fitz was soliciting when he stated, "Something you might think about is why the Midas people chose that name." In making that statement, Fitz was encouraging

---

6. *Ibid.*, p. 18.

students to attend to that relationship. Larchmont, too, turned to soliciting during the teaching episode related earlier in the chapter. "And how will I mix my paint?" "Does it have to be just white?" "Anyone want to make a fast try?" "Eric!" "Any questions?" "Get to work!" are all solicitations. Some call for a physical response as: "Get to work!" Others call for an active verbal response as: "Does it have to be just white?"

As these examples indicate, solicitations can be formulated as imperative and declarative statements as well as questions. A teacher may say, "I want everyone back in his seat," which is a declarative statement; he may direct, "Keep your voices down!" which is the imperative form; or he may ask, "Have you planned where your painting is going?" which is in the interrogative. However, regardless of their grammatical form, solicitations share a common feature: the solicitor expects a response.

Teacher solicitations can be analyzed in a number of different ways. First, an observer can study a teacher solicitation and identify whether all pupils are being directed to respond, whether any one pupil is free to respond, whether one pupil has been specified as answerer before the task has been identified, or whether the answerer is identified after the task has been stated.[7]

Teachers in the lower elementary grades frequently solicit in a manner that communicates that a unison response is expected. In a phonics exercise the teacher may direct, "Let's read this list of words that begin with a /k/ sound: *kite, cat, cake, coat, car, king, kind*"; and the children read the words orally together as the teacher points to the words on the chart. In this way all students have the opportunity to make an overt oral response; they become contributors rather than engagers. Similarly lower-grade teachers will say: "When you're ready, I want to see you sitting up tall and looking at me." The utterance is directed to all students and asks for a physical rather than a verbal response.

This type of solicitation is seen rather infrequently in upper grades. There, solicitations asking for a unison response tend to be limited to general instructional commands, such as: "Hang your paintings on the clothespins," or "Consolidate your paints."

Bellack's research indicates that teachers are more likely to identify specific respondents than to ask for a unison response.[8] Larchmont did this when he chose one student to answer his ques-

7. Bellack, *The Language of the Classroom*, p. 95.
8. *Ibid.*, p. 130.

tions about the paint; he opted for the framework in which he identified the task and then called on a respondent rather than the reverse pattern of naming the respondent and then identifying the task. Much has been written on these two solicitation patterns. Many writers suggest that stating the task before identifying the respondent has a greater chance of keeping all students cognitively involved in the task; conversely, naming the participant before stating the task can be a way of "calling back" the attention of a student whose attention is lagging or of implying that the expert opinion of a particular student is being sought.

At times teachers leave the respondent field wide open—neither indicating a particular respondent nor asking for a unison response. Small-group discussions in which youngsters and teacher are cooperatively working out solutions and, of course, one-to-one exchanges are settings in which this form of solicitation move can be observed.

The Bellack system further differentiates between solicitations that are substantive and those that are instructional. The teacher can ask or direct students to perform a task associated with the subject content under consideration; in this case the solicitation is substantive. In contrast, the teacher can call for the performance of a verbal or nonverbal task associated with classroom management; in that case the solicitation is instructional.

This distinction is a relatively easy one to apply in analyzing classroom discourse. In Larchmont's art lesson, instructional solicitations include: "Keep your voices down," "Hang your paintings on the clothespins," and "Consolidate the paint"; substantive solicitations focus directly on the art content: "Do you think it needs more white?" and "How will I mix my paint?" Analysis of the numbers of solicitations that fall into each category gives some indication of the time actually spent on matters directly related to the learning; the analysis can supply data on which the teacher can base a judgment as to whether he is spending an excessive amount of time on managerial activities.

A third way of differentiating among kinds of teacher solicitations is to identify the type of behavior called for. Does the solicitation ask for a verbal response? a nonverbal response? both verbal and nonverbal responses? Interestingly enough, Bellack found that the high school teachers he studied "almost always" asked for a verbal response.[9] Nonverbal responses expressing sub-

---

9. *Ibid.*, p. 130.

stantive meanings as defined in Module 4 were elicited relatively infrequently.

This writer hypothesizes that solicitations calling for non-verbal responses occur more frequently in elementary classrooms. Elementary teachers are prone to have young children come to the board to underline an answer, to have "everyone who thinks *yes* raise his hand," to have a child put the card in the appropriate spot or to point to the location on a map. As Bellack's work suggests, the high school teacher relies little on such devices; the high school teacher is more likely to ask the student to explain what should be underlined, where the spot on the map is, where the card should be placed—with the teacher making the related nonverbal motion. The result, of course, is that the high school student has less opportunity to move around the classroom than does the lower-grade child.

A fourth distinction among solicitations made by Bellack and his associates relates to the extent to which a student constructs the answer or selects an answer from among teacher-given options.[10] Some teacher solicitations ask for a *yes* or *no* response:

> Do they grow pineapples in Hawaii?
> Have you found your book?

Some solicitations suggest alternatives other than *yes/no* from which the respondent is to choose:

> Do you want to listen to the tape now or shall we wait till after lunch?
> Did the Spanish tend to settle in the northern or southern sections of North America?

Still other solicitations ask the student to put together a response:

> When shall we listen to the tape?
> Where did the Spanish settle?

This distinction is significant especially in analyses of class discussions. *Yes/no* and multiple-option solicitations ask students to select from among given options; on the other hand, solicitations asking for construction of a response—particularly a verbal response—require students to select an answer from within their total understanding of the topic. In this respect, answering the latter type of solicitation may require considerably more cognitive involvement than answering the former type.

---

10. Bellack, *The Language of the Classroom*, p. 98.

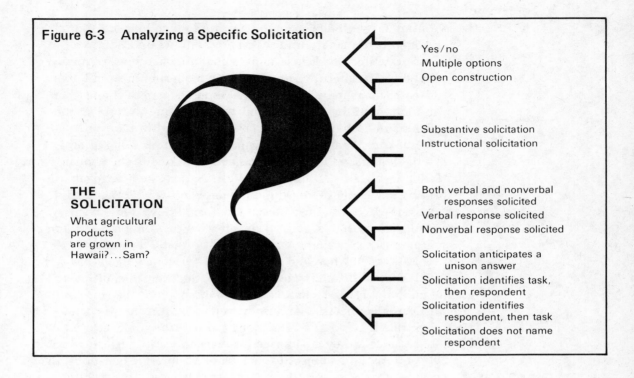

Figure 6-3   Analyzing a Specific Solicitation

THE SOLICITATION

What agricultural products are grown in Hawaii?...Sam?

Yes/no
Multiple options
Open construction

Substantive solicitation
Instructional solicitation

Both verbal and nonverbal responses solicited
Verbal response solicited
Nonverbal response solicited

Solicitation anticipates a unison answer
Solicitation identifies task, then respondent
Solicitation identifies respondent, then task
Solicitation does not name respondent

Using these four distinctions, a teacher can consider his own soliciting style: "Do I tend to—

Ask unison-type questions, questions in which I name the respondent before identifying the task, questions in which I identify the task before naming the respondent, questions in which I allow anyone to respond?

Spend most of my class time on substantive solicitations? instructional solicitations?

Solicit verbal responses? nonverbal responses? both verbal and nonverbal responses?

Ask for a *yes/no* answer? choice from among options? open construction?

Additionally, the individual teacher or teacher-intern can distinguish another aspect of his soliciting style, his soliciting repertoire—the specific words, sentence patterns, and overall approaches that characterize a teacher's soliciting behavior. A teacher may find a tendency to repeat words and phrases. This may be intentional as in the case of the elementary school teacher who uses "Miss Jones is waiting for you. She's not going to wait much longer," to tell her students to pay attention. Miss Jones draws upon that set phrase at key points. Her students know they had better "snap to"; the phrase almost elicits a conditioned response from the students. This may be unintentional as in the case of the teacher who found that she was repeating "Can anybody tell me" at the beginning of each question.

In like manner, the teacher may find that his solicitations take the imperative form ("Look here," "Take out your books," "Tell me who . . .," "Describe how . . ."), take the interrogative form ("How many of you think the answer is five?" "Where did we go wrong?"), or take a declarative form ("Miss Jones wants you to get into your seats.")[11] The teacher may find a reversal of typical sentence patterns. "How do we do that?" becomes "We do that how?" "Where did that happen?" becomes "That happened where?" A similar device found in teacher solicitations is the fill-in-the-blank technique with an inflexion of the voice indicating the final blank: "And Mary went _____?" "The person responsible is _____?" The upward life of the voice on *went* or *is* tells students they are expected to respond. Although the grammatical purists may object to such ways of phrasing questions, the sentences do communicate. In classes that this author has observed, students appear to understand what the teacher wants; they get the message. However, teachers who find through analysis that they are overusing one type of sentence pattern—all directives, all reversed sentences—may want to experiment with additional patterns.

Responding

Whereas structuring and soliciting moves are initiatory, responding is reflexive; a response is a reply to another's solicitation. By definition, responding moves are elicited by and follow solicitations.[12]

Consider the following segment of interaction:

Ms. Trippit: Can someone tell me how we convert an improper fraction to a mixed number?

Student: What you do is you divide the denominator into the numerator. But why does that work?

---

11. Bellack, *The Language of the Classroom*, p. 102.
12. *Ibid.*, pp. 18-19.

Ms. Trippit: It works because a fraction tells you how many parts you have. 25/4 tells you how many fourths you have. A mixed number tells . . .

The teacher's first utterance is a solicitation asking for a verbal response. The student responds, but continues by asking for more information. The teacher's second utterance is a response to the student's solicitation.

Responding moves can be categorized much in the manner of solicitations since responses are related directly to soliciting moves. Responses can be studied to determine whether they are

> substantive or instructional (for example, related to subject matter content or managerial activity)
>
> verbal or nonverbal
>
> *yes/no*, multiple-choice, or constructive

In the previous example of classroom discourse, both Ms. Trippet's and the student's responses were substantive, verbal, and constructive.

Bellack's research on the language of the classroom indicates that responding—at least among the high school teachers in his sample—is not a frequently made teacher move. Only 5.5 percent of the moves made by the teachers in the Bellack sample were responses. This reflects the fact that students in the classes studied did relatively little in the way of soliciting—since responses are reciprocals of solicitations. Whereas soliciting appears to be a teacher move, responding appears to be primarily a student move in the classroom game.[13] Of course, these data reflect what is happening, not necessarily what should be happening, in those classrooms. We can rightly ask, "Should students be raising questions and taking more of an initiatory role?" We can ask: "Should teachers be playing a more reflexive role?" The answers to this type of question involve value judgments, going beyond the limits of descriptive research.

Reacting

Reacting moves are defined as utterances that serve to

a. "modify" and/or

b. "rate (positively or negatively) what was said in the move(s) that occasioned them."[14]

---

13. *Ibid.*, p. 47.
14. *Ibid.*, p. 19.

Like responding moves, reactions are reflexive; they occur in conjunction with other moves. Unlike responses, however, reactions do not answer or fulfill the expectations of solicitations; rather previous moves "serve only as the occasion for reactions" and do not actively elicit reactions.[15]

A teacher modifies when he clarifies, synthesizes, or expands upon what has already been said. For instance, after a student's response that identifies the part played by public opinion in controlling environmental pollution, the teacher may repeat in slightly different words what the student has said: "Yes, public opinion has a regulatory effect"; or he may go on to elaborate the point made: "Public opinion is expressed through the press, through letters to legislators, through militant action"; or he may add: "We also must consider the part played by regulatory agencies." In each case, the words serve a reacting function.

Utterances that rate also are reactions. "Not bad for a first try!" and "Some of your stuff is good" are reactions that rate. Similarly, teachers are reacting when they interject: "You forgot the major point," "Splendid!" "Not quite," "Well, perhaps that is true under some circumstances."

A teacher's reaction can be described rather systematically by identifying components of the reaction. These components include

an explicit rating (such as *excellent, no—that's wrong, sure, fine*)
a repetition of the preceding utterance that was the occasion for the reaction, and/or
an elaboration upon the preceding utterance involving the addition of more information, the synthesis of several points, and/or the modification of the point made

Suppose a teacher reacts with "Good. You have it. The main factor is our balance of payments; but we can't forget the effect that inflation has on balance of payments." This teacher's reaction can be described as explicit rating, repetition, and elaboration. Conceivably, a reaction can be just a repetition, just an elaboration, or just an explicit rating—or any combination of the three.

Perhaps a comment should be made at this point about the effects of teacher repetition of student utterances. In the past, educators have generally spoken negatively of the practice, suggesting that teacher repetition of student comments causes students not

---

15. Bellack, *The Language of the Classroom*, p. 19.

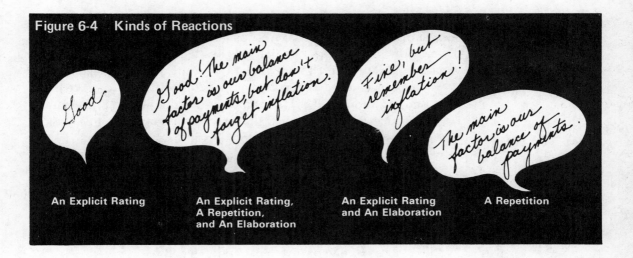

Figure 6-4   Kinds of Reactions

| An Explicit Rating | An Explicit Rating, A Repetition, and An Elaboration | An Explicit Rating and An Elaboration | A Repetition |

to listen to statements of their peers. However, categorizing these repetitions as reactions may imply that repetition serves a basic pedagogical function; the repetition is a simple way of indicating approval. Instead of saying, "Yes, that is right," which serves only to rate, the teacher repeats, thereby emphasizing and rating the point simultaneously. In this way, the teacher's words serve a dual purpose.

Research evidence is beginning to indicate that the way a teacher reacts to student statements affects student attitude toward the teacher as well as student achievement. Reviewing the related research, in the *Encyclopedia of Educational Research*, Flanders and Simon conclude that "the percent of teacher statements that make use of ideas and opinions previously expressed by pupils is directly related to average class scores on attitude scales of teacher attractiveness."[16] In other words, teachers who use praise and who make statements indicating acceptance of student ideas are more likely to be perceived positively by their students than teachers who use fewer statements of this kind. Based on this evidence, it is possible to hypothesize that perhaps teachers who repeat student statements and elaborate upon them are showing acceptance and may end up building positive student attitudes toward themselves as teachers.

16. N. A. Flanders and Anita Simon, "Teaching Effectiveness: A Review of Research 1960-66." in R. L. Ebel (ed.), *Encyclopedia of Educational Research* (Chicago: Rand McNally, 1970), p. 1426.

Sarcastic reactions made at the expense of another individual Flanders classifies as nonaccepting and criticizing. When a sarcastic reaction is made as a joke that releases tension and is not directed at a single student who must bear the brunt of it, sarcasm is classed as encouragement.[17] The distinction is one difficult to make in actual situations, but it is an important distinction to make. In the past, educators have implied that sarcasm has no place in a classroom, but as Flanders' way of looking at teacher talk proposes, not all sarcastic "joking around" is necessarily bad; rather sarcasm and joking may serve to release tension. This was true in the Larchmont case. Larchmont took the pressure off Eric with a sarcastic reaction to the class's snickering: "Your first try may not set the world on fire either," and with a sarcastic follow-up remark, "All I need is thirty-two flower pictures." The humor here was not achieved at the expense of one or several students' feelings.

As with other pedagogical moves, a teacher's typical reaction pattern can be mapped. An observer can begin by identifying the typical form of the reaction: explicit rating, repetition, elaboration. The observer can go on to ask: "Are there certain words and phrases that the teacher employs so often that they have become part of his reacting repertoire?" To find out, the observer can listen to classroom interaction on tape or on site and list all the words and short phrases the teacher used to rate student responses. Next the listing can be transformed into a tally chart. Listening again to segments of interaction, the observer can tally each instance in which the rating word was used. Specific words used numbers of times are part of the teacher's reacting repertoire.

The same type of analysis can be performed less formally by teachers in action; as teachers communicate, they can think about the reacting words they repeat. If they find an overreliance on *good*, *excellent*, *yes*, *no*, *OK*, they may want to take time to list thirty expressions they can use to communicate a positive reaction, thirty expressions to modify student answers not entirely on focus.

Activities for Encountering Pedagogical Moves

1. In a class in which you are observing, record examples of teacher statements that fulfill the pedagogical purposes described by

---

17. N. A. Flanders, *Analyzing Teaching Behavior* (Reading, Mass.: Addison-Wesley, 1970), p. 34.

Bellack—structuring, soliciting, responding, reacting. Discuss your examples with colleagues to see whether they agree with the way you classify examples. Doing this will make you more aware of the different functions performed by statements.

Initiatory	Reflexive
Structuring	*Responding*
Soliciting	*Reacting*

2. Listen to a tape of your own teaching. Concentrate on your structuring utterances and identify

   a. Words or phrases you tend to repeat as you structure
   b. Sentence patterns that typify your verbal activity
   c. Your overall structuring style—Do you jump in or move in?

3. Using the information developed in activity 2, map your own structuring approach:

Words or Phrases I Tend to Repeat:	Sentence Patterns that Typify My Structuring:

My Overall Structuring Style:

Then judge your structuring approach by asking

a. Are there words or phrases I overuse to the point they annoy listeners?
b. Do I jump in too quickly? move in too slowly?
c. Are the sentence patterns I use unclear?
d. Are my structuring moves overly lengthy and wordy? Am I getting nonverbal feedback signaling restlessness?
e. In general, do students appear to understand the who, what, why, how of what they will be doing? Again nonverbal feedback can communicate lack of understanding.

4. Select a topic or an activity to introduce to a group of students you teach. Think about how verbally you could launch that

activity or topic. Plan three different verbal approaches (they need not be long), and try them out on tape without students present. Listen to the tape, or share it with colleagues. Analyze the contents of your structuring moves as to whether participants were identified, time dimensions were specified, reasons for study were given, kind of activity was given, procedures were stated. Not all these elements are included in each structuring move; the teacher's job is to select which elements to include. Be ready to explain why you structured as you did.

5. Check youself as you lead a discussion. Do most of your questions require a *yes/no* answer, choice from among options, or construction of an answer? Tape a session and analyze your solicitations more precisely, as shown in the table below. If you find that most of your questions ask for *yes/no* responses, experiment in future sessions with other types of questions.

	Tallies	Total of Each Type
Yes/No	⦀⦀ ⦀⦀ ⫽	12
Multiple-option	⦀⦀ ⦀⦀ ⦀⦀ ⫽	16
Construction	⦀⦀ ⦀⦀ ⦀⦀ ⦀⦀ ⫽⫽⫽⫽	24

6. As you teach, experiment with solicitations that require a nonverbal response from students. If possible, study a videotape of your classroom interaction to determine if most of your solicitations ask for a verbal response.

7. As you teach a class, experiment with the patterns for solicitation: unison response, open response, student participant named before task identified, task identified before student participant named. Identify conditions under which each of these patterns works most satisfactorily for you.

8. Listen to a tape of your classroom language. Identify specific words, phrases, or language patterns that seem to typify your soliciting style.

Specific Words or Phrases Repeated in Solicitations	Language Patterns That Typify Solicitations

Judge whether this repetition is hindering communication.

9. Keep in mind that teacher responses are elicited by student solicitations. Study samples of your own classroom interaction. Do you find that you make few responding moves? If so, see if you can structure future sessions to trigger student questions—converting you into a responder and students into solicitors.

10. As you teach or listen to a tape of your teaching, see if you can identify facets of your reacting style: Ask yourself

    a. Do I tend to—
        rate, repeat, elaborate?
        rate?
        rate, elaborate?
        repeat?
        repeat, elaborate?
    b. How often do I build student comments into the ongoing discussion?
    c. How do I use sarcasm? Do I direct it at an individual? Use it to release tension?
    d. What specific words do I use to rate student responses? Is the list of rating words I use short? lengthy?

11. If you find that you draw upon a small group of words for
    reacting, consciously vary your reactions as you teach. Similarly,
    if you find that one pattern of reaction (see 10a) predominates
    in your teaching, experiment with other patterns to see if
    others might be useful as well.

BUILDING QUESTIONING SEQUENCES

In *Thinking in Elementary School Children* (Taba, Levine, and
Elzey), Hilda Taba states that the teacher's "way of asking questions
[is] by far the most influential single teaching act."[18] Taba proposes
two reasons in support of her statement. First, "a focus set by the
teacher's questions circumscribes the mental operations which students can perform, determines which points they can explore, and
which modes of thought they learn."[19] In this respect, the teacher's
questions determine whether students will be cognitively involved
in X rather than in Y subject matter.

Second, the teacher's style of questioning determines the
freedom students have to pursue related areas and to move into
other logical operations.[20] A teacher's question can be closed, cir-
cumscribing precisely the kind of thinking required and allowing
little opportunity for students to change the level of thinking called
for by the teacher. In contrast, a teacher's question can be open,
allowing students to respond "in terms of their own perceptions"
and to move into thinking operations not outlined exactly by the
teacher.

That the questioning act is a significant component of teaching
is further indicated by the work of Arno Bellack. He found that
46.6 percent of all moves emitted by teachers in his research sample
were solicitations. In terms of actual time spent in talk, the teachers
did more soliciting than they did structuring, reacting, or responding.[21] Bellack's term *soliciting* is, of course, more inclusive than the
term *questioning*. Soliciting includes verbal moves that trigger verbal, physical, or cognitive responses; they can take the form of
interrogative, declarative, or imperative utterances.

As both Bellack and Taba point out, solicitations set cognitive
tasks for students. The teacher who solicits:

---

18. *Thinking in Elementary School Children*: Cooperative Research project No. 1574.
Hilda Taba, Principal Investigator, with Samuel Levine and Freeman F. Elzey. San Francisco
State College, April, 1964. "The research reported herein was supported by the Cooperative
Research Program of the Office of Education, U.S. Department of Health, Education, and
Welfare.
19. *Ibid.*, p. 53.
20. *Ibid.*, p. 54.
21. Bellack, *op. cit.*, p. 47.

Tell me who the president of the United States is?

What is the definition of a noun?

How many pints in a quart?

What are the criteria we listed yesterday for analyzing a poem?

How do we find square root?

is asking students to recall—to emit specifics, rules, criteria, procedures from memory.

Other types of solicitations elicit higher levels of thinking described in Module 5. A solicitation such as "Describe the cloud pattern you see forming outside" asks students to reflect on what is going on around them. "How are these two samples similar?" asks students to compare. "How do they differ?" asks students to contrast. "Which is a limerick?" asks students to classify. "Which happened first?" asks students to put items in a sequential order. "Why did the Pilgrims strike out for the new world?" asks students to explain. These kinds of questions can call forth thinking beyond recall if occurring within a context of activities in which students are finding out.

Sequencing Questions

Hilda Taba has investigated questioning patterns that carry students beyond recall. Her research deals primarily with three thinking operations: grouping and classifying information; interpreting data and making inferences; and applying known principles and information to predict, hypothesize, and explain.[22] Taba and associates have identified the component elements in each of these logical operations and the sequence of steps necessary for mastering each operation:

Grouping and classifying
include:

1. Differentiating the specific properties of things; for example, listing or enumerating specific examples of a phenomenon as when young children list all the jobs that must be done in a classroom

2. Grouping together related items, as when young children group together washing boards, wiping counters, cleaning desks and group together leading the flag salute, leading the line to the auditorium

3. Labeling each category distinguished as when children apply labels to their categories: clean-up jobs, leadership jobs

---

22. Taba, *op. cit.,* p. 30.

Interpreting data and making inferences (induction)
   include:
   1. Assembling the data or specifics on which the generalizations will be based, as when students list several instances in which a specific word is used
   2. Relating aspects within the data, as when students study the examples and note that in each case x is true
   3. Formulating generalizations and inferences, as when students generalize that a specific word generally is used under x conditions

Applying previous knowledge to new situations (deduction)
   includes:
   1. Assembling related information and establishing the conditions under which a prediction is applicable
   2. Predicting what will happen
   3. Supporting the prediction with a stated or implied principle[23]

According to Taba, the steps in these cognitive operations are hierarchical. For instance, differentiating the specific properties of things represents a lower level of abstraction than does grouping together related items. Furthermore, Taba proposes that mastery of a higher-level task (labeling) requires ability to carry out tasks at a lower level of abstraction (differentiating and grouping).[24]

Taba's research bears out this hierarchical relationship. Taba studied the questioning-response patterns in elementary social science classrooms. She and her associates coded all teacher and student utterances as to whether the utterance focused the thought, extended the thought on the same cognitive level, or lifted the thought to a higher level. The levels used were those summarized in the previous section. Taba found that when teachers and students tried to lift the discussion to more abstract levels without preliminary interaction at lower levels, the solicitation did not work; the discussion did not continue at the higher level but reverted to the initial level. Only when students had first been involved at lower levels of cognition was the lift effective, the discussion continuing at the higher level of abstraction.[25]

What this research basically is telling the classroom teacher is that questions must be sequenced from less to more abstract to eventually get students operating at higher thought levels. Questions must begin with seeking information. Only when sufficient

---

23. Summarized from Taba, *op. cit.*, pp. 199-201.
24. Taba, et al., *op. cit.*, p. 35.
25. *Ibid.*, pp. 127-130.

information is available does the teacher move youngsters into grouping operations and only when youngsters have had some opportunity to group related items does the teacher emit questions that ask students to label.

The same is true of inductive thinking. Students must begin by assembling data—the specifics on which a generalization will be based. They cognitively must handle numerous specific items before being asked to develop relationships and to formulate generalizations. In a science class, for example, students can put a dry cloth into a glass, turn the glass up-side-down, and plunge it into a container of water. The students discover that the cloth does not get wet. Now they submerge an up-side-down glass into water; they hold a piece of rubber tubing up into the glass and suck in on the tubing, watching as the level of the water in the glass rises. Next they submerge an up-side-down glass into water and tilt it slightly. They observe bubbles gurgle up into the water from the tilted glass. It is only after youngsters have encountered these specific examples that the teacher, who wants students to build inductive thinking skills, moves to higher levels and asks youngsters to relate and generalize. "Why didn't the cloth get wet?" "Why did the level of the water rise as we sucked in on the rubber tubing?" "What conclusion is suggested by the bubbles that came gurgling up?"

A similar sequence is inherent in teaching for deductive thinking. Youngsters must first build inductively toward generalizations by working with specific instances—for example, the three investigations on the presence of air in the glass. When they have discovered the generalization for themselves, they turn to other related situations—lowering a straw into water. The questions now establish the parameters of the new situation: What are the features of the new situation? Under what conditions did the water previously enter the glass? Does the new situation resemble the previous ones? What conditions in the new situation differ from the previous situations? And finally, a question asks for a prediction: Will the water enter the straw? to what level? Can you support your hypothesis with reasons?

Each of the three cognitive operations investigated by Taba starts with consideration of specific items or qualities. Even in the case of deductive sequences, the first step is to consider the dimensions of the new situation to see if the generalization previously

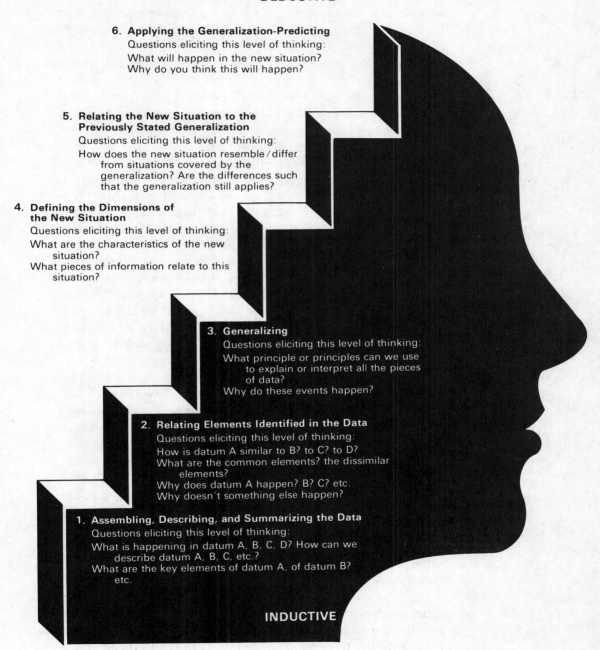

DEDUCTIVE

6. **Applying the Generalization-Predicting**
   Questions eliciting this level of thinking:
   What will happen in the new situation?
   Why do you think this will happen?

5. **Relating the New Situation to the Previously Stated Generalization**
   Questions eliciting this level of thinking:
   How does the new situation resemble / differ from situations covered by the generalization? Are the differences such that the generalization still applies?

4. **Defining the Dimensions of the New Situation**
   Questions eliciting this level of thinking:
   What are the characteristics of the new situation?
   What pieces of information relate to this situation?

3. **Generalizing**
   Questions eliciting this level of thinking:
   What principle or principles can we use to explain or interpret all the pieces of data?
   Why do these events happen?

2. **Relating Elements Identified in the Data**
   Questions eliciting this level of thinking:
   How is datum A similar to B? to C? to D?
   What are the common elements? the dissimilar elements?
   Why does datum A happen? B? C? etc.
   Why doesn't something else happen?

1. **Assembling, Describing, and Summarizing the Data**
   Questions eliciting this level of thinking:
   What is happening in datum A, B, C, D? How can we describe datum A, B, C, etc.?
   What are the key elements of datum A, of datum B? etc.

INDUCTIVE

Figure 6-5   Steps in Inductive and Deductive Thinking

stated is relevant. This gives a clue to the teacher who wants to build interactive sequences in which students begin to think at higher and higher levels of abstraction. Start with questions that focus on specific components; use those as a base on which to build more abstract questions that guide students to process the information.

This is true even with youngsters who are involved in inventive thinking, thinking in which the content is more imaginative than real or logical. Brainstorming in groups can supply the concrete data on which stories or poems are later built. If the youngsters are going to write a ghostly, haunted story, before they leap into invention, they emit specific words and phrases. The teacher encourages this perhaps through a firsthand encounter—listening to Walt Disney's record "Sounds of a Haunted House." The teacher asks for words that describe the sounds of a haunted house, and students call out their responses as a recorder writes the words or phrases on the board. "How would a haunted house look?" might be the next question, and again youngsters emit descriptive words in response. And next: "The smells of a haunted house?" "What are some reasons people would go into a haunted house?" "What could happen in a haunted house?" When lots of data have been collected, only then do students move to story writing, drawing on the data amassed.

Teachers who want to help students in formulating opinions can build similar types of experiences that move from the less to the more abstract. Teachers help students to identify needed information. "How many people were killed when the United States dropped the A-bomb on Hiroshima?" "How many people do the experts say would have been killed if the United States had had to mount an invasion of mainland Japan?" "How long had the war gone on?" "What were the conditions in Japan at the time? in the United States?" "Is it ever right to take an action that will hurt large numbers of people? If you think so, under what conditions?" These are questions that could be used as a base for the eventual value question: "Should the United States have dropped the atom bomb on Japan? Why or why not?"

In evaluative thinking, students can likewise begin by considering relevant dimensions of the item being evaluated: "How is plot developed in this short story?" "What specific techniques does the author use to develop character?" "How specifically does the

writer manipulate words?'' Only when these data have been assembled, do students make the jump into judging and then by comparing
the data assembled to previously stated criteria—a listing of characteristics of good short stories. If the particular short story in question possesses these predetermined characteristics, the story may
be judged positively.

The sequence of questions that guides students to higher levels
of abstract thinking need not be delivered orally by the teacher to
a total class of students. With the trend toward individualized and
small-group instruction, the questions can be presented through
diverse media. The teacher can put a sequence of questions and
related activities on tape. Youngsters individually or in groups can
listen to the tape, shutting off the tape after each question, thinking about the question, and formulating answers. Answers can be
discussed with others in a small group, written down by youngsters
working individually and shared later with other students who have
responded to the sequence, or even spoken onto another tape to
be compared with tapes made by other students working individually.

When students begin to get the feel for thinking patterns in
which they move from the less abstract to the more abstract, the
teacher may find that the students know the questions to ask. Instead
of the teacher's asking the questions that focus thinking at higher
and higher levels, the students begin to solicit. To get students to
question, the teacher can begin by soliciting: "What question should
we ask next?" or "What are the questions we should raise?" Only
when the students assume the role of questioner is the teacher certain that the students can carry on the cognitive operations independently.

To get students to raise questions that move thinking from the
concrete to the abstract, individualized activity is again applicable.
Students are given the ultimate question—perhaps in written form
on a ditto sheet:

Should the U.S. have dropped the A-bomb on Japan?
Write a story about ghosts, goblins, and haunted houses.
When will water enter a vessel lowered into the water?
Is short story Y a good one?

Instead of responding to the question or directive, youngsters list
all the subquestions that must be answered before they can formulate an opinion, write the story, solve the problem. The same can be

done as a subclass activity. The ultimate question can be flashed across a screen by an overhead projector; students in groups identify the questions that must be asked before the ultimate question can be answered and write those questions on an overhead transparency for future sharing with the total class. Eventually, the questions can be combined into a composite transparency.

Teachers can learn to pose questions that systematically lift student thinking to more abstract levels. This was shown in Taba's study of thinking in elementary school children. There, teachers worked for ten days to develop skill in questioning strategies that lead students from specifics to abstractions. After becoming familiar with the theory underlying the three teaching strategies outlined in this module, the teachers not only tried out the strategies but analyzed tape scripts of their actual questioning sequences. Taba later judged that "even ten days can make a marked impact on the methods of teaching" provided that the training includes both consideration of theory and opportunity for actual try-outs, feedback, and analysis of try-outs.[26] The same is probably true of techniques to get students to pose questions.

Sequencing Activities

Assuming that a teacher judges it important for students to experience questions that take them above recall and to raise questions that guide their own learning, how does the teacher begin to develop learning sequences that achieve these goals? Interactive analysis supplies a starting point. The teacher or teacher-intern might first analyze student statements using the techniques developed in Module 5. While listening to tapes of his own teaching or even while teaching, the teacher can try to identify

> student statements representing thinking at the recall level
> student statements indicating that students are involved in reflecting, relating, projecting, valuing, and/or inventing
> student statements that are initiatory—in which students pose questions

Such an analysis provides a description of the cognitive functioning of students in his classroom.

From there, the teacher can go on to plan sequences of activities that will guide students into additional thinking operations. The stress here is on activities rather than on questions, for to pre-

---

26. Taba, et al., *Thinking in Elementary School Children*, p. 67.

plan more than a few key questions is almost impossible. The activities planned can be modeled on Taba's analysis of thinking strategies. The teacher starts by considering ways to involve youngsters in information gathering so that they have a collection of specific items, examples, conditions on which to build categories, generalizations, inferences, predictions, judgments, stories. The second series of activities planned involves students in data processing or relating. These are activities that involve students in comparing and contrasting information, in asking questions about the data assembled, in relating components of the data, in organizing the data. The final series of activities takes students beyond the data to generalize, label, conclude, predict, invent—in short, to abstract.

In sum, the overall framework for planning learning sequences is:

1. Data gathering
2. Data processing
3. Abstracting

This framework—based on steps in thinking—differs considerably from a teaching scheme in which the teacher begins by telling the students the principle, the labels, the conclusion, the hypothesis, the meaning and then goes on to have youngsters supply examples.

How does the Taba-based model function in practice? Several examples may clarify:

Example 1: A vocabulary-building session

Data Gathering—Students who have heard the new word used previously will supply sentences in which the word is used; the teacher can supply additional examples to the listing.

Data Processing—Students look at each sentence trying to figure out the meaning of the word as it is used in the sentences, comparing its use from one sentence to the next.

Abstracting—Students put together a definition that incorporates the meanings they have identified in the data processing phase of the operation.

Example 2: A study of levers

Data Gathering—Students carry out a series of related experiments such as shifting the fulcrum point on a lever so that the length of the applied force arm gradually exceeds the length of the lever arm. They carefully record the force necessary to move a particular weight at each applied force arm length.

Data Processing—Students note relationships within the data. They compare the force necessary when the force arm was 1 foot long, 2 feet long, 3 feet long.

Abstracting—Students hypothesize the rule of levers—that the length of the
applied force arm determines the amount of force required to move the
weight (older students can work toward a mathematical statement of the
principle by considering mathematical relationships).

Example 3: A study of local government

Data Gathering—Students in a brainstorming session list all the kinds of tasks
that must be tended to by local governmental bodies; for example, main-
taining schools, maintaining local roads, checking violations of local
ordinances.

Data Processing—Students identify relationships among the tasks and suggest
people who would need to be employed to perform the tasks.

Abstracting—Students propose a scheme for running local government so that
all the tasks that need to be done will be responsibly carried out.

Once the teacher has planned a sequence of activities using the
data gathering/data processing/abstracting format, he has a guide
for the questions to ask when he actually teaches the lesson to a
class or subclass. Or if the teacher is moving toward an individualized system of instruction in which the traditional lesson plan is
not applicable, he has a guide for structuring questions that appear
on a written sheet or an audiotape that he prepares for students.
For instance, a tape based on the vocabulary-building session given
in Example 1 may open with the following instructions:

Listen to the following sentences: *Alice began by learning the rudiments of
grammar. Because Jack did not understand the rudiments, he could not go on
to the more difficult parts. We only considered the rudiments of the problem;
we never got into more complex considerations. After one week, only the
rudiments were visible; we saw no signs of complex growth.* Now listen again,
focusing on the word *rudiment.* In each sentence, substitute another word or
words that could be used instead of rudiment(s). Write your words on the
study guide that accompanies the tape.

After you have listed all the words that can substitute for *rudiment,*
use those words to construct a definition of *rudiment.* Compare your definition to one developed by your study partner, and if possible, rewrite your
definition to make the definition more clear.

This abbreviated "script" for an individualized tape can be easily
transformed into a written study guide. The guide can be used by
students working together in subclass teams.

In practice, of course, it is unnecessary to complete an entire
sequence of data gathering/data processing/abstracting in one
"sitting." Especially with younger children, short episodes that
are cumulative and that are interspersed with other activities

appear to be effective if the appeal of Sesame Street-type programs are any indicator of what children enjoy. On the Sesame Street-type programs, children are bombarded with related pieces of information; they may hear the /ey/ sound in a multitude of contexts—contexts that are interspersed with songs, films, jokes on diverse subjects. But more and more /ey/ sounds recur until the child puts together the pieces about the /ey/. This suggests that information or data gathering does not have to immediately precede information processing. For young children, rapid-fire encounters with related information in varying contexts and at different time periods may be called for. Abstraction comes after a period of incubation when the individual child puts the pieces together.

The same may be true of older students. An entire time block may be dedicated to data gathering; it may be several days later that students begin to process the data.

—Taba warns that techniques for involving students progressively at higher and higher levels of cognition are time-consuming. Telling students a principle and having them echo it back require much less time than completing a data gathering/data processing/abstracting sequence. In Taba's words: "As long as the expectations of teachers are focused on the final answers, rather than on the evolving thought the pacing required to develop the appropriate skills and thought forms seem intolerably slow."[27] Yet final answers are quickly forgotten if they are not based on understanding; and telling—although less time-consuming—does not necessarily develop higher-level thinking skills. Basically for the teacher to master the form of classroom communication that leads students sequentially from lower to higher levels of cognition requires a commitment to the importance of teaching students to reflect, relate, project, value, and invent. For a teacher with the commitment, time so spent is productive. In this respect, the teacher's goals and objectives are highly significant.

Timing

Researchers have recently begun study of the relationship between wait-time and the type of question asked. Wait-time is the period between the end of one participant's remarks and the beginning of another participant's remarks. Wait-time, or response time as it is sometimes called, differs from resumption time, which is the length

---

27. *Ibid.*, p. 66.

of the pauses occurring within talkspurts of a speaker; wait-time represents the pauses occurring between talkspurts of different speakers.

Mary Budd Rowe has studied the effect of wait-time on teacher utterances. Reporting at the Conference on Science and Man in the Americas held in Mexico City in June and July 1973, Dr. Rowe indicated that a change in the distribution of question types occurs "once average wait-times of three seconds or more have been achieved." She found that in a sample of science teachers, 82 percent of all questions asked by the teachers fell into a category she termed *informational;* 13 percent she categorized as *leading questions* and 2 percent she found to be *probing.* When teachers had received training in pausing (for three or more seconds) after asking a question to allow students some time to think, informational-type questions dropped to 34 percent, whereas leading questions went up to 36 percent and probing questions increased to 28 percent.[28] This research appears to indicate that when teachers pause to allow time for thinking about questions, they tend to change their questions from those calling for recall to those calling for higher-level thinking.

Most wait-time studies have been based on audiotapes of classroom interaction. It is interesting to hypothesize possible relationships between pauses in verbal interaction and nonverbal communication—something generally not recorded in the studies. In *Rhythms of Dialogue* Joseph Jaffee and Stanley Feldstein report a study in which wait or response time of two inter-reactors was clocked when visual-gestural clues were available and compared with response times that occurred when all visual-gestural clues were blocked by a curtain separating the two. When visual-gestural information was blocked out, response or wait-time decreased.[29] Because with blockage of nonverbal information, wait-time decreases, it seems plausible to hypothesize that pauses between speakers are periods when nonverbal communication supersedes verbal communication. In classrooms, longer wait-times may be eliciting additional nonverbal teacher clues that encourage youngsters to ponder and that reward nonverbal considering behavior by students.

28. Mary Budd Rowe, "Science and Future Control," a speech given June 27, 1973, at Science and Man in the Americas, American Association for the Advancement of Science, Mexico City.

29. Joseph Jaffee and Stanley Feldstein, *Rhythms of Dialogue* (New York: Academic Press, 1970), p. 42.

The Rowe study and the Jaffee and Feldstein investigation may lead the reader to conclude that increasing wait-time is something for which to strive. This, however, would be only partly valid. Teachers who have worked with restless groups of youngsters know from experience that it is important to keep the pace up. Lags in activity may result in lags in attention. Perhaps the distinction here is between lags in activity and momentary pauses lasting about three seconds and placed at points in a discussion that definitely call for sophisticated thinking. That momentary pause used at definitive points can tell students not to jump into a fast answer but to consider interrelated factors. Shorter wait-times may have their place during the information-gathering phase of a question sequence. By varying wait-time, the teacher can communicate to the students some clues about the kind of thinking necessary in putting together a response.

Activities for Developing Questioning Strategies

1. Write questions that ask students to perform the thinking operations listed in the chart on page 148. Describe the context in which you would use each question to insure that it carried students beyond recall. For instance, the question "How many pints in a quart?" calls for recall if students are giving back information read; it calls for generalizing if students have poured pints of water into a number of different quart containers to find out.

2. When you work with students to build understanding of concepts, do you systematically move from the concrete to the abstract? To answer this question, study an audiotape of your classroom interaction. Identify specific points in your talk, when you

   a. told students a generalization they could have discovered themselves
   b. gave students information that they could themselves have identified as being relevant in that context
   c. asked students for a generalization, inference, prediction without building a base of information on which to make the generalization

   If you find such examples, list them, and discuss with other teachers or interns how you could have designed the activity so that students are involved systematically in the discovery of concepts.

The Thinking Operation	The Question	The Context
a. Describing		
b. Summarizing		
c. Comparing		
d. Grouping related items		
e. Labeling		
f. Explaining		
g. Generalizing		
h. Justifying		
i. Predicting		

(Activity 1)

3. Plan several sequences of activities on which you could base classroom questions that lead students from data gathering to data processing and to abstracting. If you are an elementary school teacher, select the content of each sequence you design from a different subject area in the curriculum. If you are a secondary school teacher specializing in one discipline, select each sequence from a different area within the discipline. Use the following format in your planning:

    Activities to involve students in data gathering—
    Activities to involve students in data processing—
    Activities to involve students in abstracting—

4. Imagine yourself in a class guiding students in a small group through one of the sequences you designed in activity 3. What questions might you use to trigger each phase of the involvement? *Question* is used here loosely to include any kind of solicitation.

5. Try out at least two of the sequences developed in activity 3 with a subclass, a class, or an individual student. Tape your try-out for later analysis. Later, listen to the tape, list all the questions you used in order, and identify questions you were using to lift the thinking to higher levels of abstraction. Decide whether you got students thinking beyond recall.

6. Prepare a written study guide for use by a group of students. In designing the guide, start with questions that call for data gathering; then move to questions or activities that require data processing and abstracting.

7. Prepare an audiotape for use by an individual student based on the principle of sequencing questions and activities from lower to higher levels of abstraction. The student can perform the activity or answer the questions by writing, by responding into the recorder, by performing a series of tasks, by talking to another student who has listened to the tape.

8. Experiment with varying your wait-time. When you ask a question that you are certain goes beyond recall, extend the time that you wait before accepting an answer. When you ask a fact question, cut the wait-time. Do you see differences in the kind of answer students give to you? What nonverbal devices do you use during the wait-time?

9. Listen to yourself on audiotape as you teach a lesson. Consider—

    a. The speed with which you talk:

        Do you vary the speed depending on the kind of response you are looking for?

        Do you vary the speed depending on the difficulty of the subject matter?

        Do you vary the speed depending on the restlessness you read from students' nonverbal clues?

    b. The way you handle time within and after your talkspurts:

        Do you pause within your talkspurts to emphasize, to gain attention, to leave room for nonverbal clues you want to emit, to indicate a change of topic?

        Do you appear to vary your wait-time? If so, what factors seem to be determining the length of time you wait before accepting a response?

MODULE 7
Encoding
Nonverbal
Messages

MODULE GOALS

The teacher gains competency in—

categorizing gestures, eye movements, use of distance and touch as encouraging or restrictive and in using body language that encourages

using nonverbal expressions to indicate participants, react and respond to participants, focus attention, gain attention

using nonverbal expressions to emphasize and illustrate

manipulating materials in ways that are in accord with his intended message

controlling his personal motions, especially nonverbal mannerisms

using a variety of nonverbal expressions

describing his own nonverbal style

Mr. Gonzales leaned forward in his chair. Pulling at his chin, Gonzales focused intently on Marcie, one student in a group of four with whom he was discussing the group's project activity. Marcie was describing to him how the group intended to present its project investigation to the class. As Gonzales listened, his expression changed from thoughtful consideration to enthusiastic acceptance. Only once did a slight frown cross his face; as Marcie hastened to re-explain, the frown disappeared.

When Marcie had completed her explanation, Gonzales nodded approvingly, stood up, sauntered toward his desk, picked up a book, sauntered back, opened the book, and held it so the group members could see. "Here is another way of presenting data," he said, pointing to a time line on the page. At that point, Gonzales glanced at Sam, who had made a slight joining motion, and gestured at the boy. Sam asked whether in their case the line could be drawn as a spiral to show the effect of the inventions being plotted on the expanding life style of the people. Gonzales responded with an enthusiastic nod and a wide smile, verbally adding, "It might work; try several sketches. Perhaps Jack can design for you." That he was pleased with the idea showed now in his broad grin and relaxed manner.

Then Gonzales pulled on his chin, sat back in his chair, and thought for a moment. Pointing to the tape recorder in the corner, he queried, "Thought about taping some of your findings?"

The youngsters shook their heads. Marcie replied, "We thought we'd stick to transparencies to report to the class."

Gonzales didn't react; he was gazing across the room at a group of three boys who were fooling around. Gonzales made a wide gesturing motion with his arm in the direction of the boys. When he got no return signal, he stood up abruptly, strode over, surveyed each participant with a long look and said, "Hey fellas— this isn't a locker room!" He stood looking down for a moment, letting his gaze move sternly from one face to the next. He slowly shook his head and added: "Get back to work." Before he turned, the slightest smile crossed his face—a smile that almost said, "You're good kids."

Returning to the first group, Gonzales pulled down his sweater, settled into his chair, grinned apologetically as if to say, "Sorry for the interruption," and directed, "Repeat that, Marcie." And Marcie repeated her remark.

GOING BEYOND WORDS

A listener to an audiotape recording of Gonzales' interaction with his students obviously would have missed much of what Gonzales was "saying." Without perceiving the nonverbal clues Gonzales was emitting, the listener might have gained the erroneous impression that the teacher was nonaccepting and nonencouraging of student ideas and feelings, for Gonzales made no verbal statements that praised or encouraged, none that accepted student feelings, and none that fully expressed complete acceptance of student ideas.[1] Gonzales did not tell Sam, "Great idea"; his words suggested only tentative approval: "It might work." He did not react verbally to Marcie's report with a statement of acceptance; rather he suggested other alternatives. With the three boys, Gonzales' words were abrupt; and even when he returned to the work group, his words were directive: "Repeat that, Marcie."

Clearly Gonzales was not relying on words to communicate his approval, concern, and liking; he was relying on nonverbal clues. His face told when he was pleased with an idea; the focus of his eyes and body indicated where his thoughts were and where he wanted students to look; the tension of his body muscles told when he was relaxed; his nod communicated a go-ahead signal and his pause communicated a let's-stop message.

---

1. Ned Flanders, *Analyzing Teaching Behavior* (Reading, Mass.: Addison-Wesley, 1970), p. 34.

It is also clear that Gonzales' students read the messages that
he sent nonverbally. They knew that his smile and nod were his
signs of pleasure; they worked for those signs. They knew that a
long gaze meant displeasure. They probably recognized that Gonzales
was not prone to rate verbally—that he let his body react for him.
And then, of course, there was the way he pulled at his chin; Gonzales' students doubtlessly knew that this gesture meant little.
Gonzales was always doing that and was not even aware of his
mannerism.

The Emotional Meaning

In *Teaching Is Communicating: Nonverbal Language in the Classroom*, a publication of the Association for Student Teaching,
Charles Galloway stresses the fundamental role of such teacher nonverbal clues in encouraging or restricting communication. He proposes that nonverbal expressions range from those communicating
enthusiastic support, intention to help, and receptivity to pupil
talk, to those communicating inattentiveness, unresponsiveness,
and disapproval. In the Galloway system for categorizing the emotional message sent through nonverbal clues—

Enthusiastic support	means	"Enthusiastic approval, unusual warmth, emotional support or strong encouragement."
Helping	means	"A spontaneous reaction to meet a pupil's request, help a pupil, or answer a need. A nurturant act. . . . An action intended to help."
Receptivity	means	"Willingness to listen with patience and interest to pupil talk."
Pro forma	means	"A matter of form or for the sake of form . . . neither encourages nor inhibits communica-tion. A routine act. . . ."
Inattentive	means	"Unwillingness or inability to be attentive. Disinterest or impatience with pupil talk."
Unresponsive	means	"Failure to respond when a response would ordinarily be expected. Egocentric behavior, openly ignoring need, insensitive to feeling."
Disapproval	means	"Strong disapproval, negative overtones, dis-paragement, or strong dissatisfaction . . . physical attack . . . utterance suggesting unacceptance, disappointment, depreciation, or discouragement."[2]

2. Charles Galloway, *Teaching is Communicating: Nonverbal Language in the Classroom*
(Washington, D.C.: Association for Student Teaching, 1970), pp. 11-12. Copyright 1970
by Association for Student Teaching; reprinted by permission of the publisher.

Using these seven categories, the teacher or the observer can make inferences about the emotional message sent by teacher nonverbal clues and the influences this message has on student perception. Galloway writes that "when teachers have had the opportunity to study their own nonverbal patterns, their first response is amazement—that their own behavior can make such a difference. They are struck by the lasting influence it has on student understanding and perception."[3]

The components of the message that have such a lasting influence on student perception include:

Gestures	motions of hands, arms, torso, feet, face, head; the nod, smile, grimace, wave, kick are the "words" of gesture. A wide smile can be interpreted as enthusiastic support; a frown or a pointed finger that threatens can send a message of disapproval; a waving gesture can signal receptivity to student remarks as the teacher encourages the participant to continue talking.
Eyes	the focus and appearance of the eyes. Eyes can, for instance, look bright and attentive signaling receptivity to student talk; they can look "far away" signaling inattention. Changes in eye focus communicate; sudden shifts signal shifts in thought, concentration, interest.
Stance	aspects of posture that communicate attention, tension, weariness, and the like; also such sudden shifts in position from slumping to sitting upright, standing to moving can signal shifts from unresponsiveness to responsiveness or vice versa.
Touch and distance	movements that close or extend the distance between pupil and teacher—extending the hand toward, touching as in patting, leaning toward are signals of support and receptivity; drawing back physically, striking, leaning away can signal inattention, unresponsiveness, disapproval.
Speed of motion	the rapidity with which movements are made; motions made with haste can communicate concern or lack of concern dependent on the situation. Motions made slowly similarly must be interpreted within context.
Vocal effects	the loudness/softness, high pitch/low pitch, tone, voice quality of speech. Vocal inflection can signal the full range of emotions.

The Substantive Message

These components of nonverbal language communicate not only an emotional message; they have substantive meaning as well. For this reason, teacher nonverbal expressions can also be categorized as to the instructional tasks being performed. Barbara M. Grant

---

3. *Ibid.,* p. 11.

has identified three distinctive instructional tasks that teachers perform nonverbally in classrooms: conducting, acting, and wielding.[4]

As explained by Barbara Grant and Dorothy Hennings in a Teachers College Press publication, *The Teacher Moves: An Analysis of Nonverbal Activity*, "a teacher physically conducts a class by involving one, some, or all of his students" in an interaction. In conducting, the teacher emits gestures, uses eyes and stance, manipulates distance and touch to "control student participation and obtain attending behavior."[5]

According to *The Teacher Moves*, a teacher is controlling participation when he uses nonverbal expressions to accomplish the following tasks:

> To indicate participants by smiling at, focusing eyes on, orienting body toward, nodding at, pointing at, walking toward, touching a participant.
>
> To react to a participant by using expressions of the face (a frown, a grin), shaking and nodding the head, patting the child to express approval, making signals such as OK with the fingers, shrugging the shoulders, moving hands to brow, holding hands in a way that shows pondering.
>
> To respond to a participant by shaking and nodding the head, moving toward or away from the participant, pointing.
>
> To focus attention by pointing, moving and holding up objects, writing an answer on the board, moving toward an object or participant, shifting gaze or stance.[6]

A teacher is obtaining attending behavior when he uses nonverbal language

> To gain the attention of members of the class by walking to a key position in the classroom, striking an object to make a noise, opening a book such as the roll book, picking up an object such as a paintbrush, maintaining a physical posture, surveying the classroom, making eye contact with a series of students in sequence.
>
> To gain the attention of one or more inattentive students by orienting his body in the direction of the student(s), by walking toward, touching, making hand gestures, changing facial expression, shaking head.[7]

---

4. Barbara M. Grant, "A Method for Analyzing the Nonverbal Behavior (Physical Motions) of Teachers of Elementary School Language Arts," unpublished doctoral dissertation, Teachers College, Columbia University, 1969, pp. 41-43.

5. Barbara M. Grant and Dorothy G. Hennings, *The Teacher Moves: An Analysis of Nonverbal Activity* (New York: Teachers College Press, 1971), p. 11.

6. *Ibid.*, pp. 93-97.

7. *Ibid.*, pp. 97-99.

Although conducting motions occur when a teacher is conducting the class as a whole, they also occur when the teacher works with individuals or groups. The teacher working tutorially with a youngster may point to focus attention on a map that the student is making, to react to the student's work product, to respond to a question. Similarly the teacher may use gestures to gain the attention of a single child who is working independently and with whom he wants to confer.

In *The Teacher Moves*, acting refers to body motions used to emphasize, illustrate, or amplify.[8] A teacher is emphasizing when he makes gestures of hand, head, face, torso, legs, feet that heighten the impact of his words or other nonverbal signals he is emitting. He emphasizes too when he moves quickly toward something in which he is expressing interest. He emphasizes when he assumes a stance or an eye focus that adds heightened impact.

A teacher is acting when he emits motions that illustrate. Illustrative motions attempt to clarify or make more explicit the meanings a teacher is communicating. Illustrative motions help to clarify elements in the communication process as when the teacher finishes a statement and comes to a physical halt that says, "I am finished talking. It's your turn to answer."

Illustrative motions differ considerably in size and extent. The teacher in talking about "back and forth" may simply sway his fingers gently in simulation of a back-and-forth rhythm. Or the teacher can opt for a role playing clarification in which he uses his whole body to illustrate a concept or an act; he may pretend he is riding a horse and let his entire body bounce up and down as he talks about what it feels like to ride a horse.[9]

In the Grant system, the third teaching task accomplished through nonverbal language is wielding. In wielding, the teacher makes motions in reference to objects, materials, or parts of the classroom environment. He manipulates materials such as books, pens, pencils, maps, projectors, erasers, globes. Additionally, he scans, looks at, surveys, or reads these materials and makes motions that facilitate his manipulation or survey of materials.[10]

Typically the teacher does not emit wielding motions in order to communicate with students; he emits wielding motions as

---

8. *Ibid.*, pp. 12-13.
9. *Ibid.*, pp. 12-13.
10. *Ibid.*, pp. 13-15.

he prepares the materials for instruction. However, regardless of the teacher's intent, wielding motions send messages to students just as clearly as the pursuing motions emitted by students send significant messages to the teacher. The speed with which the motion is carried out, the teacher's preoccupation, the teacher's stance and eye focus tell students much about the teacher's interrest in the task, state of well-being, concern about time and neatness. Just what the teacher is wielding—maps, overhead projector, chalk—also supplies the students with clues about what they might be expected to do.

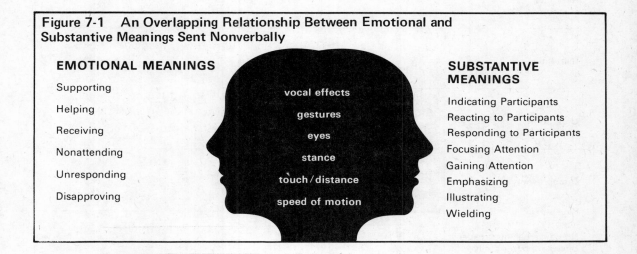

Figure 7-1   An Overlapping Relationship Between Emotional and Substantive Meanings Sent Nonverbally

EMOTIONAL MEANINGS

Supporting

Helping

Receiving

Nonattending

Unresponding

Disapproving

vocal effects

gestures

eyes

stance

touch/distance

speed of motion

SUBSTANTIVE MEANINGS

Indicating Participants

Reacting to Participants

Responding to Participants

Focusing Attention

Gaining Attention

Emphasizing

Illustrating

Wielding

Activities for Analyzing and Trying Out

1. Study a videotape of your own teaching activity. Focus on your use of gesture, distance, touch, stance, and eye movements. Analyze your body language on Galloway's continuum of nonverbal performance from encouraging to restrictive. At approximately thirty-second intervals, rate the nonverbal expression you see yourself using. Place a tally in the appropriate box along the continuum. Study the data you amass, and make a judgment about the impression you are creating with your body language.

Emotional Messages	Tallies	Total
Enthusiastically supportive		
Helpful		
Receptive		
Inattentive		
Unresponsive		
Disapproving		
No nonverbal message per-ceived at point of tally		

Note: if you have no access to videotaping equipment, pair
with another teacher or teacher-intern. You observe your
colleague for several fifteen- to twenty-minute intervals.
Tally for each other, and talk together about your findings.

2. If your analysis suggests that your body language tends toward
the restrictive, consciously make an attempt to focus seriously
on what students are saying. Work at not letting your mind
wander. Of course, you cannot really feign interest, but it may
be possible to reorganize classroom activity to make it more
interesting to both you and your students.

3. Observe in a classroom, and identify the specific messages the
teacher is sending through the "vocabulary" of nonverbal

communication. Write down specific examples of messages
sent through each form of body communication; with colleagues, talk about the impact that these messages have on
student participants:

"Vocabulary" of Nonverbal Language	Examples of Specific Messages Sent Nonverbally
Gesture	
Eyes	
Stance	
Touch and distance	
Speed of motion	
Vocal effects	

4. Begin to work on your use of body language to perform the nonverbal teaching tasks. As you teach, think about the way you typically tend to indicate participants, react to participants, and the like. Focus on one of these tasks for several days until you have a clear concept as to how you use nonverbal language for that task. Then develop a composite description of your nonverbal teaching language, using the following format:

Conducting Motions—motions I use to
Indicate participants
React to participants
Respond to participants
Focus attention
Gain attention of participating students
Gain attention of nonattending students
Acting Motions—motions I use to
Emphasize
Illustrate
Wielding Motions—characteristics (fast/slow, decisive/indecisive and the like) of motions I use to
Manipulate materials
Survey or look at materials
Prepare to manipulate materials

Once you gain a concept of how you use nonverbal language for each of these tasks, experiment with nonverbal expression. For instance, if you find that you seldom use gestures that emphasize, "try some motions on for size."

5. Read Part II of *The Teacher Moves* (New York: Teachers College Press, 1971) by Grant and Hennings and Chapter 3 "Improving Nonverbal Language" in *Teaching is Communicating* (Washington, D.C.: Association for Student Teaching, 1970) by Galloway.

CONSIDERING NONVERBAL TEACHING STYLE

The word *style* has been used by numbers of writers to refer to the overall manner in which a teacher teaches—to the teacher's typical way of using body, distance, space, time, and, of course, words.

Tendency to Use Body Language

One facet of a teacher's distinctive style is his tendency to communicate physically, to use body language to take the place of words or to complement his words. In analyzing this aspect of his style the teacher considers:

Do I ever let my body communicate the entire message? Do I ever turn off my verbal commentary?

Do I use nonverbal expressions to complement my words? If so, are my actions congruent with my words?

Do I tend to use my body to emphasize and clarify verbal meanings or do I tend to rely on words to get my emotional and substantive messages across?

Do I ever use complete physical and verbal silence to carry my message?

How expressive are my eyes and face? Do my eyes and face express helpfulness and support? Is my face ever a dead pan?

Does my stance complement my verbal message?

In sum, do I have a nonverbal orientation toward communication? a verbal orientation? a verbal/nonverbal orientation?[11]

Certain instructional advantages accrue to the teacher who has a tendency to use nonverbal expressions. A shift from verbal to physical communication can add interest and variety.[12] Students who have been listening with their ears must begin to "listen" with their eyes, and the often incessant teacher voice disappears at least

---

11. Grant and Hennings, *The Teacher Moves*, p. 43.
12. *Ibid.*, pp. 76-77.

momentarily from the classroom. A shift from verbal to physical communication can also speed up the pace. A simple nod can take the place of a lengthy sentence. Instead of repeating, "Does anyone else have anything to add?" after each student comment, waiting for a show of hands, and then naming a respondent, the teacher can use eye focus to ask for other opinions and nod at students who show they want to join in. Increased clarity of communication may be a third bonus. The teacher who wants to tell students how to do something can demonstrate the process often more clearly and rapidly than he can explain verbally; the teacher who wants to indicate shape, size, or location can similarly express these meanings more clearly with simple hand gestures that accompany a verbal utterance.[13] Fourth, a nonverbal message can be sent while a verbal interaction is in progress. A teacher who notes that a student has become inattentive or distracting can send a conducting motion to obtain attending behavior even as the class continues with its substantive work. In so doing, the teacher does not interrupt the ongoing activity and does not make the disruptive youngster the center of attention.

Then, too, as Galloway points out, nonverbal expressions are particularly effective carriers of emotional meanings. The smile, the reassuring nod, the leaning toward can tell a student, "You're OK," or "I'm interested in you," or "Great piece of work!" The extended look, the frown, the fast shake of the head, the pulling physically away can communicate the opposite meaning. In these contexts, "actions do speak as loud as words—perhaps, louder."[14]

Teachers of young children may find that body language is an especially vital form of communication to use. Young children rely particularly on gesturing to get their messages across. A three-year-old will point to answer; vocalization complements the gesture. Later, when communication demands grow more complex, the child must rely more fully on verbal language to communicate. Then gestures begin to complement words.[15] As a result, in working with young children, teachers may find that they must rely more heavily on the language of motion and action that plays such a significant part in children's communication systems. They may

13. *Ibid.*, pp. 76-78.
14. Charles Galloway, "Nonverbal Communication," *Theory into Practice*, vol. 7, no. 5, December 1968, p. 172.
15. Frederick Williams, "Acquisition and Performance of Communications Behaviors," in Larry Barker and Robert Kebler (eds.), *Speech Communication Behavior* (Englewood Cliffs, N.J.: Prentice-Hall, 1971), p. 113.

find that they must act out meanings and be more physically expressive and active than they tend to be in adult communication. Thus, any judgment about whether a particular teacher is using sufficient nonverbal clues is dependent on the age level of the students with whom he is working.

Just as limited use of nonverbal clues can be a problem that teachers identify in their own teaching style, so also can excessive use be a second problem. Complete stillness—a cessation of both verbal and physical language—has its place in the classroom. Stillness can serve to heighten an effect, allow time for thought, or signify a change of focus. A teacher who is a ball of nonverbal activity may fail to take advantage of the communication potential of stillness. Likewise, a teacher may so overuse nonverbal language that it ceases to have meaning. Gestures no longer serve to emphasize or illustrate; they may even distract or overstimulate.[16]

A third problem relates to the correspondence between verbal and nonverbal statements. Because a teacher uses nonverbal expressions to complement words, an incongruity between the verbal and nonverbal messages may occur. According to Galloway, "congruity occurs when the teacher's verbal message is supported and reinforced by nonverbal behaviors to the extent that there is consonance between verbal intent and nonverbal referents. A mixed message or incongruity exists when there is a discrepancy or contradiction between the verbal message and nonverbal information."[17] For example, the teacher may react to a youngster's work with a "Very nice." Yet his face may be telling the youngster, "I had hoped for more" or even that the teacher was considering something else and was making a perfunctory verbal remark.

Body language that is incongruent with verbal utterances can give away a teacher's hidden prejudices and preferences. Herbert Koch speaks of the way in which students identify children who are teacher's pet. The teacher may say that he likes all students equally, but nonverbal language belies the words. Eye movements, stance, and gestures indicate which children are favorites; whether he gets physically close and touches a student adds to the message.[18] The same is true of other prejudices. The teacher may verbally say:

---

16. Grant and Hennings, *op. cit.,* p. 78.
17. Galloway, "Nonverbal Communication," *op. cit.,* p. 174.
18. Herbert Koch, "The Teacher and Nonverbal Communication," *Theory into Practice,* vol. 10, no. 4, October 1971, p. 234.

"Cleaning up is fun"; but his actions are saying, "I hate to clean up."

Tendency to Rely on a Limited Nonverbal Repertoire

A second facet of a teacher's style is the specific nonverbal expressions that recur. In analyzing this aspect of style, the teacher considers:

> How do I tend to respond and react? Do I rely on specific gestures such as a nod? a smile? a movement of the shoulders?
>
> How do I typically focus attention: by pointing? by walking toward? by holding up an object?
>
> How do I typically emphasize: by pumping my hand up and down? by nodding my head as I speak?
>
> What verbal statements do I repeat, accompanied by a set nonverbal expression (such as "You know what I mean" accompanied by a waving gesture of the hand)?
>
> How do I indicate participants: by pointing? by nodding? by walking toward?
>
> What illustrative gestures recur in my teaching?
>
> What is my typical way of manipulating materials? What materials do I tend to manipulate?

A teacher may discover a tendency to repeat a specific gesture of hand, foot, head, body, and/or face. In reacting, he may smile and nod to indicate a positive rating, frown and shake the head to indicate a negative rating. Because these expressions recur in the teacher's performance, they are integral components of that teacher's style.

Similarly, in responding, a teacher may rely on one or two specific gestures to complement verbal statements. One teacher may be a pointer—gesturing with the hand to tell where. In soliciting, that teacher may point as well—using the hand to indicate participants and focus attention. Even in structuring, the teacher may find that a recurring nonverbal expression is the hand gesture of pointing. In this respect, nonverbal structuring, soliciting, and responding repertoires are restricted.

A teacher who discovers a limited nonverbal repertoire may find it profitable to consider the numbers of ways to substitute other actions for the recurring one. Instead of pointing, the teacher can hold up the object, walk toward it, lean toward it, touch it. This is the same thing a teacher tries to do when discovering an overuse of a specific word; he seeks other word substitutes.

Position/Motion Tendencies

A third aspect of nonverbal teaching style is the teacher's typical manner of moving and holding his body:

> The position in which the teacher tends to hold his head, torso, arms, hands, feet—the question: Are there one or two positions of head, torso, arms, hands, feet that characterize my teaching stance?
>
> The overall position the teacher employs—the questions: Do I tend to sit, stand, lean as I teach? What kinds of activities are standing activities for me? sitting activities? leaning activities? When I stand, where do I position myself? When I sit, what kind of chair do I select?
>
> The general activity pattern—the questions: Do I commonly remain in one position as I teach? Do I tend to move as I teach? Do I cover large/small distances as I teach?
>
> The typical size of gesture—the questions: Do I tend to employ large-sized gestures? small-sized gestures?

Research has not shown that there is one correct position for teaching or one general activity pattern that is most effective. Research tells us only that each teacher has a distinctive manner of using position and motion in teaching. The teacher who knows his style, however, is in a better position to evaluate the effects of the components of his style on students and systematically to build a teaching style that is successful.

Going beyond description, the teacher can begin to ask the interpretive question: What am I communicating through my stance? my motion patterns? Am I communicating relaxed self-control? nervous indecision? active involvement? disinterest? As previously noted in Focus Two, "there's a way you walk, you know, when you're walking happy" and a way you walk when you're walking sad. This applies to teachers as well as to students.

Tendency to Interject Personal Motions

Another component of a teacher's nonverbal style is a tendency to emit motions of a personal rather than a pedagogical nature. According to Grant and Hennings, the teacher emits personal motions when striving to "achieve a more balanced state, . . . to release tension and to achieve a more relaxed and comfortable bodily position." Additionally the teacher uses personal motions to rearrange articles of clothing and to make physical adjustments in response to inner conditions such as an itch or a sneeze. When personal motions—or self-adjusting motions as they are also called—are repeated to the extreme, they are considered mannerisms.[19]

Teachers who view videotapes of their classroom activity are often amazed when they discover some of their own mannerisms. They may discover that they are scratchers, fiddlers, or pacers. They always seem to be scratching some part of their anatomy, fiddling with something—chalk, a pencil, a necklace, a tie—or pacing back and forth and up and down. Others may discover their tendency to keep pushing back their hair, pushing up their glasses, or even pulling on their ears. Of course, on videotape some personal motions that are fleeting become apparent—nose blowing by the cold sufferer, shirt tucking by the teacher who has worn an annoying shirt, shoe adjusting by the teacher breaking in a new pair of shoes. Clearly, it is the recurring personal motions, not the fleeting ones, that systematic analysis should uncover.

The teacher who does not have access to videotaping equipment may find it profitable to pair with another teacher for analytical purposes. Each teacher observes several sessions of the other teacher's interaction, listing each personal motion emitted by the teacher during that period. The teacher later analyzes the listing to locate nonverbal mannerisms. Interestingly enough, the teacher who knows that he is being observed for this purpose may identify personal motions while performing them. He will "catch himself in the act" of jiggling pocket coins, fiddling with chalk, or scratching, and will make an obvious effort not to complete the motion.

Vocal Tendencies

One of the significant findings of the studies reported by Joel Davitz in *The Communication of Emotional Meaning* is that people differ in their ability to express feelings vocally. Subjects in a study conducted by Phyllis Levy were given a statement relatively free of emotional content: "I am going away on a trip. I will be gone all summer long. If anyone wants to reach me, give them my address." The subjects had to repeat this statement a number of times, each time expressing a different emotion. Some were rather successful in completing the task so that listeners could perceive the emotion they were attempting to communicate; others were less successful.[20]

19. Grant and Hennings, *op. cit.*, p. 10.
20. Phyllis Levy, "The Ability to Express and Perceive Vocal Communications of Feeling," in Joel Davitz (ed.), *The Communication of Emotional Meaning* (New York: McGraw-Hill, 1969), p. 46.

The Levy study suggests that teachers probably differ in vocal expressiveness and that a facet of their style is their tendency to communicate emotional meanings vocally. The teacher interested in identifying this aspect of style can study several audiotapes of classroom talk and ask: "Can youngsters tell through my voice when I am enthusiastic, disapproving, helpful, receptive to their talk, thoughtful?"

A related aspect of style is vocal attractiveness. The teacher can ask:

Is my voice

high pitched	low pitched
soft	loud
monotonous	varied
fast	slow

and describe his voice in terms of each continuum. Clearly, at this point, the teacher must go beyond description of vocal characteristics to a judgment of quality. This is essential here, for the teacher who has gone from describing his own voice as *very* low pitched to judging his voice as *too* low pitched may be ready to take steps to change voice quality.

Activities for Analyzing and Trying Out

1. Using the questions outlined on pages 161, 164, 165, and 167, study your teaching performance as recorded on videotape. Then write a paragraph in which you describe:

    a. your tendencies to use body language
    b. the nonverbal expressions that characterize your teaching
    c. the overall motion patterns and stance that characterize your teaching
    d. your vocal characteristics

2. Study particularly your personal motions either by having a colleague list each personal motion you emit during a segment of your teaching or by listing such motions yourself as you watch yourself on videotape playback. Analyze the list to identify personal motions that have become mannerisms and may be influencing student reaction to you.

3. Study a tape of your nonverbal classroom performance to see if you can perceive your "hidden" prejudices. Look for the hidden message that is telling students that you dislike a particular subject, activity, topic, student.

4. If your analysis uncovers a tendency to rely on a limited non-verbal repertoire, list alternatives you can try out. Make a conscious attempt to try out some of the alternatives as you conduct, act, and wield.

5. If you find that your body is nonexpressive—that you infrequently use body talk to emphasize or illustrate—go back to Module 3 of this book and work on some of the activities related to freeing inhibitions to use the body to express meanings.

6. As you teach, keep in mind the mannerisms you have identified in your teaching style. Make a conscious effort not to scratch, or fiddle, or whatever.

7. If you find that your voice is rather nonexpressive, experiment with your voice. Using the statement employed in the Levy study reported on page 166, repeat it, each time expressing a different feeling. Tape your renditions. See if your colleagues can "read" the feelings you are expressing.

MODULE 8
Designing an Environment for Classroom Interaction

MODULE GOALS

The teacher gains competency in—

recognizing the effects of spatial and temporal variables on classroom communication

designing classroom space so that space-use patterns facilitate communication

designing classroom time blocks so that time-use patterns facilitate communication

Friday afternoon. 2:30 P.M. The thirty-six adolescents in George Jacobson's last-period English class sat six abreast and six deep facing him as they "discussed" the origin of words on which they had run dictionary checks for Thursday night's homework. The interaction format was typical of many high school classes. A student explained the origin of a word. Jacobson asked for additional responses. A student or two commented. Jacobson summarized, then moved to the next word and to the next student in the row for an explanation. There was little student-student verbal interaction. The "discussion" was being mediated by Jacobson. Students glanced at the clock as they almost visibly waited for the dismissal bell.

An observer that afternoon would probably have rated the lesson as perfunctory and dull. The design of the verbal interaction— a traditional teacher-question/student-response pattern based on review of homework—hardly warrants the term *discussion* and was motivating little student enthusiasm. In addition, physical factors related to the design of space and time were at work limiting the possibility of an effective discussion.

Mounting research in the social sciences and in education indicates that the design of spatial and temporal features in an environment is a significant determinant of communication patterns that develop. In short, the way time and space are organized can facilitate or limit interaction. Seen in this perspective, the physical features of classrooms assume considerable importance when one studies what goes on there.

169

SPATIAL FEATURES OF CLASSROOMS

Edward T. Hall uses the term *fixed-feature space* for those perma-
nent elements of building design that mold and organize the
activities of individuals and groups; once constructed, fixed features
cannot be shifted by participants in the activity.[1] The room plan
of a home, the design of a village, the grouping of several buildings
are organizers of activities in that they affect how people function
within the space and how they communicate with one another.

The Classroom Box

The fixed features of school space similarly influence activities and
communication. Although the designs of schools differ from one
geographical area to another and differ according to the year of
construction, most schools retain the classroom cell-unit as the
basic structural component with special service areas—library,
auditorium, cafeteria, all-purpose room, laboratories, lavatories,
gymnasium, offices—appended to supplement the cell-units. Halls
connect individual units, and are usually the sole means of access
to the classrooms.

In many schools the unit is a rectangular box. It has windows
along one wall, has chalkboards along what is generally set aside as
the front of the room, has bulletin boards and coat racks (in elementary schools) along the inside wall. Lighting fixtures hang from
the ceiling and are controlled by two or three switches. Depending
on the money spent for construction, some classrooms have additional fixed features: a built-in sink and water fountain, an appended
lavatory, a door that leads directly outside. Only in a few newer
buildings do we find movable walls or no walls at all.

The reason for the design of the traditional fixed features of
classrooms has been investigated by the psychologist Robert Sommer;
reporting in *Personal Space: The Behavioral Basis of Design*, Sommer
writes:

The present rectangular room with its straight rows of chairs and wide windows
was intended to provide for ventilation, light, quick departure, ease of surveil-
lance, and a host of other legitimate needs as they existed in the early 1900's.
Before the advent of the electric light, it often required legislative action to
compel economy-minded school boards to provide adequate fenestration. The
typical long narrow shape resulted from a desire to get light across the room.
The front of each room was determined by window location, since pupils had

1. Edward T. Hall, *The Hidden Dimension* (Garden City, N.Y.: Doubleday, 1966), p. 97.

to be seated so that window light came over the left shoulder. Despite new developments in lighting, acoustics, and structures, most schools are still boxes filled with cubes each containing a specified number of chairs in straight rows.[2]

Although the physical design of classrooms may not meet program needs of education in the 1970s and although educators may decry its existence, the design remains, perhaps because of continuing cost considerations. The educator must realize, however, that the boxlike design of classrooms molds the organization of activities carried on there as well as the form and style that communication assumes.

First, the classroom area is undifferentiated. Whereas a house has built-in areas for talking to friends, for talking to family members, for sleeping, for eating, the classroom box has no areas designed for the specialized tasks that occur there; a classroom has no alcove for individual reading, no specific area designed for informal activity or conversation. Built-in differentiation comes primarily from the placement of chalkboards; the chalkboard marks the front of the room and is the focus of student attention and the organizational point of communication activity.

Second, the classroom box has no differentiation achieved through lighting. The lighting effect is global. Perhaps just one row of lights can be used to achieve a slight change, but it is impossible in the average box to darken one area while keeping another fully lighted or to soften the overall lighting effect. The informal groupings of furniture in differentially lighted areas found in the average living room are nonexistent in classrooms; as a result, large-group interaction becomes the norm.

Because the room is fundamentally an open box, privacy is at a minimum. In the design of the room, there is no place to be alone, away from the observing eyes of others; regardless of where a person is, actions—the language of the body—are easily perceived. Then, too, communication between two or among several individuals is open to inspection. In an undifferentiated arena, privacy can be achieved only by turning the back and whispering. These actions in themselves communicate to others in the situation. They say, "This is private. Keep out!" And just as the closed door is frowned

2. Robert Sommer, *Personal Space: The Behavioral Basis of Design* (Englewood Cliffs, N.J.: Prentice-Hall, 1969), pp. 98-99. Copyright 1969 by Prentice-Hall; reprinted by permission of the publisher.

upon in some offices, so the turned back can be frowned upon as a signal of conspiracy in the classroom. Participants in an undifferentiated box have no real alternative but to allow what they say and do to be viewed by others if they do not wish to appear secretive.

The Functional Box

The problems inherent in the fixed features of classroom space can be remedied to some extent by the differentiated use of color. Basing his proposal on research indicating that reds appear to activate whereas blues and greens appear to calm, Clifford Drew of the University of Utah suggests:

Both the light-dark and hue dimensions of color may be found to be effective in space division. Activities in different areas within a classroom might be facilitated with different coloration *depending on the instructional program.* Space in which more active instruction (and learning responses) are conducted could perhaps be more workable if colored in light reds. Areas where more passive participation is desired may function better if colored in dark blues or greens.[3]

Where areas cannot be differentiated with paint, the teacher can attempt some color differentiation through construction paper pinned to bulletin boards or murals designed and executed by youngsters that can cover an area of the wall. For example, a semiprivate conversation area can be designed into a corner of the classroom simply by arranging an attractive art display in that corner and turning two chairs informally into the corner. A color scheme used on a limited portion of the bulletin board can similarly set off an area to which students go for small-group discussion activity.

Just as problems inherent in the fixed features of classroom space can be overcome to a limited extent by purposeful use of color, manipulation of what Hall calls the semifixed features of space can change the communication environment of the classroom.[4] Semifixed features include chairs and desks if they are movable, area rugs, pianos, bookcases, file cabinets, movable partitions, screens, and demonstration tables. Some privacy can be obtained by placing file cabinets, bookcases, and pianos per-

---

3. Clifford Drew, "Psychological Behavioral Effects of the Physical Environment," *Review of Educational Research,* vol. 41, no. 5, December 1971, pp. 457-458. Copyright 1971 by the American Educational Research Association; reprinted by permission of the publisher.
4. Hall, *op. cit.*, p. 101.

pendicular to the wall rather than against it. Some areas can be
designed so that a corner set off and painted a particular color is
partially shielded from the activity in the remainder of the room;
a student can seek out the corner for a period of leisurely reading
or for individual project work. A piece of carpet can be used to
differentiate areas of an elementary classroom; a rug where young
children collect to hear a favorite story sometimes serves effectively
to define an area of the room. A movable partition can similarly
differentiate a listening station from more active areas of the classroom.

The Design

Because these semifixed features of space are under teacher control,
the way the teacher manipulates them sends significant situational
messages to students. Students are quick to perceive the implications of the positioning of the teacher's desk, the overall arrangement of their desks (in rows, clusters, a circle), the presence of
listening and conversation areas constructed from outward jutting
bookcases. They know that certain designs give them more freedom
to interact whereas other designs prohibit interstudent conversation.
They know that some designs enable the teacher to keep an eye on
them even when the teacher is working with other individuals or
groups, that other designs give them greater independence.

The design, likewise, communicates the value the teacher
places on different activities. To partition off a corner of the room,
to place in that corner several comfortable chairs, to add a lighting
fixture that casts a soft, relaxing glow, and to encourage youngsters
to use the corner for recreational reading are ways of showing the
youngsters the value the teacher places on reading. The design says,
"Reading is an ideal way to spend one's free time."

Then, too, the way a teacher arranges chairs and tables in the
room encourages or discourages sharing of ideas during small-group
discussion periods. From his studies of what he calls small-group
ecology, Sommer has discovered that when students were asked to
select the kind of seating arrangement they prefer for performing
different kinds of activities, they chose the following: for conversing, students preferred a catercorner and a face-to-face arrangement rather than a side-by-side arrangement; for cooperating on a
task, students chose the side-by-side rather than the catercorner

or face-to-face placement.[5] Sommer cites research by Lorne Elkin in which children's choice of seating was studied. In Elkin's study, few young children selected face-to-face seating; the width of the table was too great a gap. With increased age, however, sitting across was chosen more, sitting side-by-side chosen less. Girls tended to select side-by-side seating more frequently than boys.[6]

Based on an analysis of numbers of studies of seating arrangements that encourage discussion, Sommer concludes that side-by-side seating is one of the least successful; side-by-side seating is useful primarily when participants are involved in a cooperative task in which they are sharing materials.[7] Sommer's conclusion is one for teachers to contemplate as they arrange classroom chairs for discussion purposes; any attempt to develop the true give-and-take of discussion with youngsters lined up in rows is more likely to result in failure than in successful interaction. Students in this arrangement are sitting side-by-side with adjacent pupils, a position that allows too little opportunity for eye contact and one that research shows is least likely to produce discussion. Of course, there is absolutely no eye contact possible with students sitting forward and back.

The traditional row arrangement appears also to affect the pattern of student participation. In classes organized in rows, Raymond Adams and Bruce Biddle have identified what they call the *action zone*. The action zone "extends from the front of the room directly up the center line, diminishing in intensity the further away it is from the point of origin."[8] Pupils sitting in this central zone emit the majority of verbal responses made by students in the class. Adams and Biddle find this to be true at all grade levels and in all classrooms investigated and tentatively conclude that the environment may have the power to "coerce" behavior. They wonder if the teacher should deliberately try to overcome the tendency to teach to the action zone and to work for heightened involvement with students in the fringe areas. They wonder whether "it is necessary to restructure the classroom environment so that different seating arrangements force a different, more eclectic pattern of communication."[9]

---

5. Sommer, *op. cit.*, pp. 62, 63.
6. *Ibid.*, p. 64.
7. *Ibid.*, pp. 61-73.
8. Raymond S. Adams and Bruce J. Biddle, *Realities of Teaching: Explorations with Video Tape* (New York: Holt, Rinehart and Winston, 1970), p. 50.
9. *Ibid.*, p. 51.

   In the upper grades, such an eclectic pattern may be achieved
by placing desks around the perimeter of the room with chairs
positioned toward the walls during individual work sessions. During
small-group discussions, chairs can be moved into clusters; during
total-class discussions, chairs can be placed informally in the center
of the room in the space freed by moving the desks into the classroom fringes. For notetaking during discussions, students have
available writing boards, which are simply pieces of plywood cut
to the appropriate size. In this arrangement, chairs and desks are
not considered inseparable units; rather chairs are mobile, to be
carried to discussion or work areas, and desks are conceived as individual study stations to be used for serious concentration.

   In the lower grades, desks may be converted into tables for
small-group activity by pushing four or six together. No longer does
a child "own" a desk; instead children keep possessions in an
attaché case-like box that can double as a stool and that they carry
from one learning station to another as they complete individual
study activities. During large-group and small-group discussions,
children squat on the floor in close clusters that make interaction
more informal. Project work is carried out at the learning stations
located at the tables.

   The teacher who contemplates adoption of any nontraditional
design is forced to modify existing communication patterns. Some
designs make impossible the question-answer format that typifies
much verbal interaction; others require a totally different approach
to the organization of classroom time. In this respect, to borrow
Adams and Biddle's term, the environment coerces teacher behavior.

   Additionally, the environment has the power to determine
physical action patterns and the physical closeness of the interaction.
In the row-by-row set-up, the teacher tends to concentrate his gross
physical movement at the center front of the class, entering what
Adams and Biddle call the *inland strip* or the *ring road* less frequently.[10] It appears plausible that other designs—clusters, perimeter
patterns, elimination of individual desks, concentric circles, radiating
patterns, rectangles—contribute to the action patterns that result in
classrooms where they are employed. Some designs mandate extensive physical movement by both teacher and pupils. Some, such as
the demonstration table placed at the front of some science classrooms, erect physical barriers between teacher and pupils, limiting

---

10. *Ibid.*, p. 37.

the closeness of the interaction. Other designs encourage close interaction.

The Furnishings

What the semifixed features are like also influences the quality of
interaction. Compare the furnishings of a classroom to those of
an average home. Most of us know the pleasure of curling up on a
comfortable, soft sofa to chat companionably with a friend. Conversation flows easily as we relax with feet up, head supported by
the high back of the sofa. In contrast, we give youngsters in school
hard, straight chairs and sit them at inflexible desks often too small
for their rapidly growing frames. We keep students on that chair for
at least four hours each day, granting them respite only during
lunch, recess, physical education, a few gamelike activities, and
passage between classes. In some schools, there has been movement
toward large tables as part of the furnishings. These are used for
reading or discussion activities, but typically students and teachers
tend not to use them as the major locus of interaction. Compare,
too, the window coverings—in schools, stiff blinds or shades, very
rarely soft draperies.

Some educators suggest that soft chairs and a relaxed atmos-
phere cause the mind to wander. How many educators, when they
have writing and reading tasks to accomplish at home, select a hard
chair for themselves? Probably few. Perhaps the real reason we continue to stock classrooms in the traditional way is cost; hard plastic,
wooden, and metal furniture can take abuse.

What do these features of classroom semifixed space do to
communication? Surely, the exchange of ideas carried on with
children or youths sitting at desks is less informal and relaxed than
a similar exchange occurring within a home; the classroom itself
"speaks" of structured, institutionalized formality and almost
forces the teacher to plan large-group activities for the total class
rather than attempting individual activities.

To overcome the strictures imposed on classroom communication, the teacher of younger children often encourages children to
gather on a rug during talk-times. Or the teacher pushes desks together into clusters to make less formal groupings and introduces
mats, pillows, and hassocks into the environment. He employs
folding tack boards to cordon off areas in the classroom so that
more intimate groupings result. Such changes can affect the quality

Figure 8-1   A Classroom Map

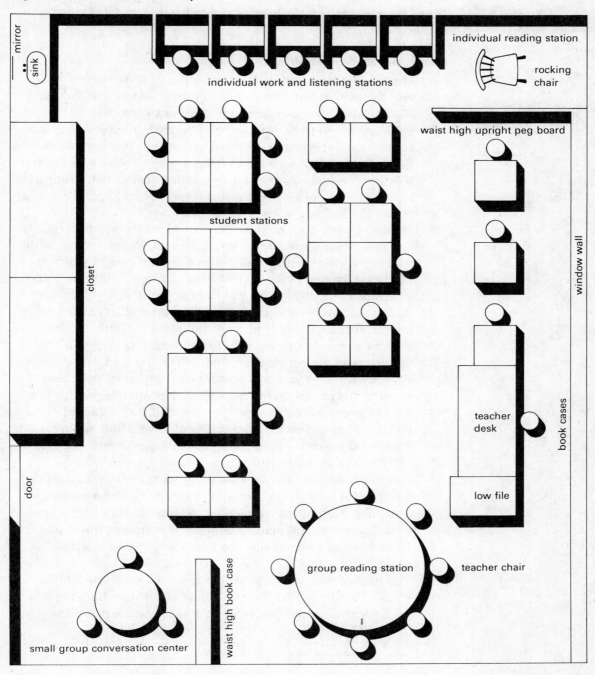

of interaction and can compensate to some extent for the institutional message sent by the unwieldy semifixed features of classroom space.

Investigating Spatial Features

1. Study the interaction pattern in a series of classrooms you visit by using a grid system developed by Adams and Biddle.[11] Mark off on a rectangular piece of paper twenty-five equal rectangular segments—five across, five down. Imagine that the twenty-five segments are marked off on the classroom floor. Each time a student makes a verbal response, place a dot in the segment representing the area in which he is located. From what areas of the room are most verbal responses emitted? That location is the action zone within the classroom.

2. Using the same grid, map the teacher's "territory," the physical space he tends to occupy in the classroom. Using a watch with a second hand, identify the spot in the classroom in which the teacher is located as the second hand marks off sixty-second intervals. Put a dot on the grid to represent the spot occupied during each sixty-second period. Is the teacher a center-front, an inland-strip, a ring-road, or a stationary person?

3. Become aware of the action zones and the territory you tend to occupy in your own classroom. When you lead a discussion, consider whether you are focusing on one part of the classroom to the exclusion of fringe areas and what territories you tend to occupy. Test yourself; have a student plot a grid of participation eminating from different areas of the room during several lessons. Upper-grade students may even be able to tell you what your territory is.

4. Draw a classroom map on which you plot the fixed and semifixed features of your classroom or of one in which you are observing. Hypothesize how these features mold communication. Draw a second map on which you rearrange the semifixed features to overcome the limitations of the original design.

5. The teacher who views classroom space as one single undifferentiated area tends to teach the class as a whole. Looking at your own classroom or a room in which you are observing,

---

11. Adams and Biddle, *Realities of Teaching*, p. 37.

consider what has been done to differentiate the classroom into functional units and what factors are at work that appear to coerce the teacher into teaching the class as a total group.

6. Identify the functions that need to be performed in your class. Then devise a plan for differentiating your classroom into areas that will serve the needed functions. You should end up with a classroom map that shows positions of desks, chairs, tables, boards, and so forth.

7. Identify situations in which you would want to limit student-student interaction. How could you employ spatial considerations to limit student-student interaction?

TEMPORAL FEATURES OF CLASSROOMS

Time has the potential to shape communication and determine the organization of classroom activities. The school day has rigid boundaries. There is a precise beginning and a precise end to the large units of time during which students are in the classroom. School may begin at 8:45; the lunch bell rings at 11:45. This schedule is known to the participants before they begin to function together; foreknowledge that the group must be ready to disperse by the predetermined moment shapes interaction.

Additional time boundaries are built into the secondary school day. Periods are forty-five to fifty-five minutes long; students must arrive at their next class within the three to five minutes allotted for travel time.

Built into the elementary school day are similar fixed features of time—features beyond the control of participants but known to them at the outset. At 9:22, the class must be ready for the music specialist; at 10:35 the children are expected at the library; at 11:07 Michael must be in the auditorium for his violin lesson. These are inflexible time slots around which a teacher must operate.

The Consequences

The consequences of the fixed features of school time are numerous. The teacher may have to cut short a girl's conversation; it is time for gym, and the girl must be told, "We'll talk later." The teacher may have to halt a group discussion that has just hit its mark and has involved a number of students. He may have to effect an abrupt change in tone or mood; students involved in a discussion on the implications of war may have to change gears so that they can burst into a stanza of "The Green Grass Grows All Around" with the newly arrived music teacher or so that they can rush off to math class. Essentially, the fixed features of time determine closure; they halt communication sequences.

The closures imposed by inflexible time schedules are a feature of schools that frustrates the student intern beginning to teach. The intern, who plans logically developed sequences allowing youngsters to discover generalizations for themselves, finds that before students have experienced all the planned activities, it is library time or that Jane must leave for remedial reading and will never encounter the discovery phase of the lesson.

In contrast, the experienced teacher has learned to modify planned activities progressively. Having pre-planned several inter-related activities and seeing the end of the time block approaching, he modifies—leaving out least essential elements, combining several activities, turning to less time-consuming techniques. In this way, there is time before the end of the period to generalize, conclude, or synthesize. In like manner, the teacher may find that the pre-planned activities do not fill the time block; now he includes enrichment activities that reinforce. To this teacher a lesson plan is not a predetermined track but rather numbers of possible experiences from which to draw flexibly.

The Unexpected

Teacher and students must similarly adjust their exchange of ideas to the unanticipated features of classroom time. At the peak of excitement about a shared idea, the fire bell rings, and the sharing comes to an abrupt halt. Adults interrupted under comparable conditions carry their exchange with them as they walk along. Not in schools! For safety, students are silent during drills. And an experienced teacher knows how difficult it is to regenerate the enthusiasm in a topic when a five-minute break has been interjected. Especially with younger children whose attention span is limited, the interrupted teacher may be forced to begin a new sequence that hopefully will bring youngsters to the high point of discovery destroyed by the bell.

Unanticipated interruptions abound in schools—the messenger sent from another class, the blare of the public address system, the visitor dropping by. If the teacher has not developed for himself a way of handling these interruptions with a minimum of distraction, they can become disruptive forces; all other exchanges stop as the teacher tends to the intrusion.

The Teacher's Schedule

Present in classrooms are semifixed features of time—features at least partially under the control of classroom participants. The secondary school teacher controls how he will organize the forty-five- or fifty-five-minute period. Likewise, although state law mandates the number of minutes per week to be utilized for certain activities, the elementary teacher generally determines the precise scheduling of those minutes. Some elementary teachers react by building additional rigidity into the time blocks already fixed into the day:

8:55-9:10	Reading Group A
9:10-9:25	Reading Group B
9:25-9:40	Reading Group C
9:40-9:45	Drink Time
9:45-10:05	Music
10:05-10:35	Arithmetic

The secondary teacher may break the fifty-five-minute block into several smaller units:

9:00-9:15	Lecture
9:15-9:25	General Discussion
9:25-9:40	Small-group Project Work
9:40-9:50	Reports

Religious adherence to such rigid patterns obviously increases the number of arbitrary closures already built into the institution. Amazingly, some administrators still expect precise time scheduling and are upset when they find a teacher off schedule. Of course, some general plan for organizing blocks of unscheduled time is needed! That design, however, should be flexible enough to permit continuation of an active discussion, to allow pairs of children to finish an exchange and to permit the teacher to listen to that little girl's conversation.

Then, too, the design of time blocks must take into account other environmental factors—time of day, temperature, number of students. For instance, last period Friday, ten minutes before lunch, ten minutes after recess are times requiring special attention; activities planned for these periods must provide for normal student restlessness.

The Message

Just as the teacher's handling of semifixed features of space communicates, the way he handles time "speaks." For example, a junior high school science teacher used the first ten minutes of a fifty-five-minute period to get out the materials needed for the class. He had no purposeful activity planned for the students during this time, but carried on an informal conversation with the students who gathered around him. When he finally started, he was plagued by student inattention. Collecting information to help the teacher, a resource supervisor spoke to the students. The youths generally expressed the feeling that they liked to talk informally with Mr. Greene but they thought that he did not believe what they were doing was important; if he did, he would be ready for them. Mr. Greene's failure to use time purposefully communicated to his class a casualness about learning that gradually infected his students; when he finally got down to business, the students had caught his covert message and had begun to think that the work was unimportant.

Contrast Mr. Greene's message with the message sent by the teacher who has several work options from which the students can choose as soon as they enter the room: study the books in the New Books Display; take your writing folder from the file and record scientific observations made on the way to school; make a summary of the class notes recorded yesterday; check in your dictionary the meaning of the word written on the bulletin board; do your classroom job—wiping up the demonstration table, adjusting blinds. In these classrooms, the youngsters catch the message: we are here to learn and do.

Investigating Temporal Features

1. In a classroom in which you are observing, list the anticipated fixed features of time. Describe verbal or nonverbal statements that indicate that these features are effecting closure. If you have your own classroom, listen to a tape of your performance and identify closure statements resulting from fixed-time features.
2. In a classroom in which you are observing, identify the unanticipated time features that affect communication. Try to identify the teacher's techniques for minimizing the effects of these variables.

3. List specific statements—verbal and nonverbal—made by a classroom teacher that communicate his view of time usage. What messages is he sending by his manipulation of time blocks over which he has control? Does his actual use of time conflict with his verbal statements about how time should be used?

4. Map your own use of classroom time:

    a. List the anticipated fixed features of time to which you must adjust. Identify ways you adapt your instruction to meet the requirements of these features.

    b. Identify ways you minimize the unanticipated fixed features of time.

    c. List additional time boundaries you build into your classroom.

    d. Interpret the messages you send by your actual use of time.

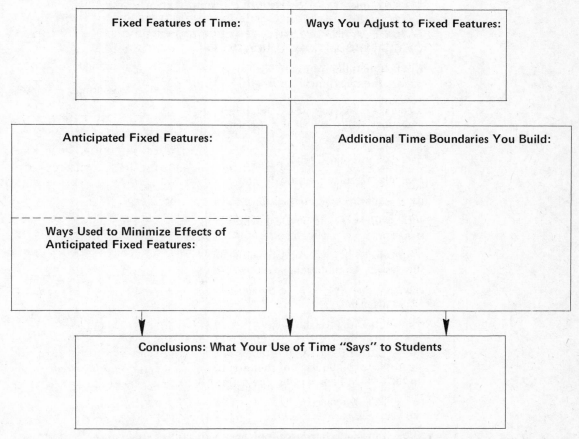

NOTE: Listening to an audiotape recording or watching a videotape recording of your typical classroom behavior may help you complete this exercise in interactive analysis.

REVIEW
Mastering
Classroom Communication

The teacher who has completed the eight modules that comprise this book may want to evaluate informally his own growth in ability to handle classroom communication processes. In review, the following composite self-analysis guide is presented as a means through which the individual teacher can evaluate his own growth toward mastery of classroom communication skills.

GUIDE FOR ANALYZING A TEACHER'S MASTERY OF CLASSROOM COMMUNICATION

I. The Communication Process: Am I able to—

	Usually	Sometimes	Rarely
recognize messages sent vocally, physically, and situationally as well as those sent verbally?			
decode nonverbal feedback?			
recognize messages sent by distance?			
use distance to send messages?			
speak with vocal and physical expressiveness?			
use words clearly with understanding of the possible connotations words carry?			
change verbal style to meet the needs of my listeners?			
control the situational messages I send?			
recognize masking behavior?			
identify the components of the filter through which I am viewing interaction?			
recognize differences in the way people perceive messages?			
recognize when others' attention has wandered?			

II. The Teacher as Receiver-Decoder: Am I able to—

	Usually	Sometimes	Rarely
describe the typical nonverbal behavior of my students?	___	___	___
perceive changes in typical motion patterns of my students?	___	___	___
interpret nonverbal student feedback, especially behavior signaling restlessness?	___	___	___
use nonverbal clues to perceive facades students construct to hide true feelings?	___	___	___
judge the effectiveness of my teaching by analyzing student nonverbal feedback?	___	___	___
approximate the amount of student talk occurring in my classroom?	___	___	___
distinguish between student statements that represent a response and statements that represent an initiation?	___	___	___
interpret what students say in terms of the thought processes represented by student statements?	___	___	___
distinguish between student statements that represent recall and statements representing higher levels of thinking?	___	___	___
accept the language patterns of speakers of nonstandard English?	___	___	___

III. The Teacher is Source-Encoder: Am I able to—

	Usually	Sometimes	Rarely
vary my use of interactive teaching formats to serve varying instructional purposes?	___	___	___
use the form of solicitation that relates most directly to the goals I seek?	___	___	___
vary my reacting moves to meet the needs of the situation?	___	___	___
build student answers and questions into my reactions?	___	___	___
structure and respond so students know where they are going?	___	___	___

	Usually	Sometimes	Rarely
plan interactive sequences and ask questions that guide students from the less to the more abstract?	_____	_____	_____
design verbal materials for small groups and individuals that are sequenced so that students begin by gathering information and move to processing information and abstracting?	_____	_____	_____
design verbal sequences in which students raise questions?	_____	_____	_____
vary wait-time dependent on the kind of thinking being solicited?	_____	_____	_____
handle diverse sentence patterns?	_____	_____	_____
use body language that is encouraging?	_____	_____	_____
use nonverbal expressions to:			
indicate participants?	_____	_____	_____
react and respond?	_____	_____	_____
focus attention?	_____	_____	_____
gain attention?	_____	_____	_____
emphasize?	_____	_____	_____
illustrate?	_____	_____	_____
manipulate materials in ways that are in accord with my intended message?	_____	_____	_____
control my nonverbal mannerisms?	_____	_____	_____
use a variety of nonverbal expressions?	_____	_____	_____
recognize the effects of spatial and temporal variables on communication in my classroom?	_____	_____	_____
design classroom space so that space-use patterns facilitate communication?	_____	_____	_____
design classroom time blocks so that time-use patterns facilitate communication?	_____	_____	_____

	Fully	Partially
describe the components of my own verbal style?	_____	_____
describe the components of my own nonverbal style?	_____	_____

Bibliography

Adams, Raymond S., and Bruce J. Biddle. *Realities of Teaching: Explorations with Video Tape.* New York: Holt, Rinehart and Winston, 1970.

Amidon, Edmund, and Elizabeth Hunter. *Improving Teaching: The Analysis of Classroom Verbal Interaction.* New York: Holt, Rinehart and Winston, 1966.

Amidon, Edmund J., and Ned Flanders. *The Role of the Teacher in the Classroom.* Minneapolis, Minn.: Paul S. Amidon and Associates, Inc., 1963.

Asch, Solomon, and Harriet Nerlove. "The Development of Double Function Terms in Children: An Exploratory Investigation," in Bernard Kaplan and Seymour Wapner (eds.), *Perspectives in Psychological Theory: Essays in Honor of Heinz Werner.* New York: International Universities Press, 1960, pp. 47-60.

Baratz, Joan. "A Bi-dialectal Task for Determining Language Proficiency in Economically Disadvantaged Negro Children," Eric Document No. 020 519, 1968.

Baratz, Joan C. "Language and Cognitive Assessment of Negro Children: Assumptions and Research Needs," *American Speech and Hearing Association,* vol. 11, 1969, p. 88.

Barker, Larry, and Robert Kebler (eds.). *Speech Communication Behavior.* Englewood Cliffs, N.J.: Prentice-Hall, 1971.

Bartlett, F. C. *Remembering: A Study in Experimental and Social Psychology.* Cambridge, England: Cambridge University Press, 1967.

Bay, Stuart, and William Thorn. *Visual Persuasion.* New York: Harcourt Brace Jovanovich, 1974.

Bellack, Arno A. (ed.). *Theory and Research in Teaching.* New York: Teachers College Press, 1963.

Bellack, Arno A., Herbert Kliebard, Ronald Hyman, and Frank Smith. *The Language of the Classroom.* New York: Teachers College Press, 1966.

Bereiter, Carl, and S. Englemann. *Teaching Disadvantaged Children in Pre-School.* Englewood Cliffs, N.J.: Prentice-Hall, 1966.

Birdwhistell, Ray L. *Kinesics and Context: Essays on Body Motion Communication.* Philadelphia: University of Pennsylvania Press, 1970.

Bloom, Benjamin. *Taxonomy of Educational Objectives: The Classification of Educational Goals, Cognitive Domain.* New York: David McKay, 1956.

Brooks, William. *Speech Communication.* Dubuque, Iowa: Wm. C. Brown, Co., 1971.

Bryant, Donald, and Karl Wallace. *Oral Communication: A Short Course in Speaking*, 3rd ed. New York: Appleton-Century-Crofts, 1962.

Burling, Robbins. *English in Black and White*. New York: Holt, Rinehart and Winston, 1973.

Cundiff, Merlyn. *Kinesics: The Power of Silent Command*. West Nyack, N.Y.: Parker Publishing, 1972.

Davitz, Joel (ed.). *The Communication of Emotional Meaning*. New York: McGraw-Hill, 1969.

Deutsch, Cynthia. "Auditory Discrimination and Learning: Social Factors," *Merrill-Palmer Quarterly*, vol. 10, 1964, pp. 277-96.

Dillard, J. L. *Black English*. New York: Random House, 1972.

Drew, Clifford. "Psychological Behavioral Effects of the Physical Environment," *Review of Educational Research*, vol. 41, no. 5, December 1971, pp. 447-65.

Ebel, R. L. (ed.). *Encyclopedia of Educational Research*. Chicago: Rand McNally, 1970.

Fast, Julius. *Body Language*. New York: Evans and Co., 1970.

Flanders, Ned A. *Analyzing Teaching Behavior*. Reading, Mass.: Addison-Wesley, 1970.

Forsdale, Louis. *Nonverbal Communication*. New York: Harcourt Brace Jovanovich, 1974.

Friend, Joseph. *An Introduction to English Linguistics*. New York: World Publishing, 1967.

Galloway, Charles. "The Challenge of Nonverbal Research," *Theory into Practice*, vol. 10, no. 4, October 1971, pp. 227-30.

Galloway, Charles. "Nonverbal Communication," *Theory into Practice*, vol. 7, no. 5, December 1968, pp. 172-74.

Galloway, Charles. *Teaching is Communicating: Nonverbal Language in the Classroom*. Washington, D.C.: Association for Student Teaching, 1970.

Goffman, Erving. *The Presentation of Self in Everyday Life*. New York: Anchor Books, 1959.

Grant, Barbara M. "A Method for Analyzing the Non-verbal Behavior (Physical Motion) of Teachers of Elementary School Language Arts." Unpublished doctoral dissertation, Teachers College, Columbia University, 1969.

Grant, Barbara M., and Dorothy G. Hennings. *The Teacher Moves: An Analysis of Non-verbal Activity*. New York: Teachers College Press, 1971.

Grim, Harriett. *Practical Voice Training*. New York: Appleton-Century-Crofts, 1948.

Hall, Edward T. *The Hidden Dimension*. Garden City, N.Y.: Doubleday, 1966.

Hall, Edward T. *The Silent Language*. Garden City, N.Y.: Doubleday, 1959.

Hayakawa, S. I. *Language in Thought and Action*, 2nd ed. New York: Harcourt Brace Jovanovich, 1964.

Hennings, Dorothy. *Smiles, Nods, and Pauses.* New York: Citation Press, 1974.

Hennings, Dorothy, and Barbara Grant. *Content and Craft.* Englewood Cliffs, N.J.: Prentice-Hall, 1973.

Hughes, Marie, and associates. *The Assessment of the Quality of Teaching: A Research Report.* U.S. Office of Education Cooperative Research Project, No. 353. Salt Lake City, Utah: The University of Utah, 1959.

Jaffee, Joseph, and Stanley Feldstein. *Rhythms of Dialogue.* New York: Academic Press, 1970.

Koch, Herbert. "The Teacher and Nonverbal Communication," *Theory into Practice*, vol. 10, no. 4, October 1971, pp. 231-36.

Kochman, Thomas. "Rapping in the Ghetto," *TRANS-action*, vol. 6, Feb. 11, 1969, pp. 26-34.

Labov, William. *Language in the Inner City.* Philadelphia: University of Pennsylvania Press, 1972.

McGaw, Charles. *Acting Is Believing*, 2nd ed. New York: Holt, Rinehart and Winston, 1966.

McLuhan, Marshall. *Understanding Media.* New York: McGraw-Hill, 1964.

Meyers, R. E. "Listening," *Grade Teacher*, vol. 88, March 1971, pp. 30-31.

Miller, Gerald. *Speech Communication: A Behavioral Approach.* Indianapolis: Bobbs-Merrill, 1966.

Montagu, Ashley. *Touching: The Human Significance of the Skin.* New York: Columbia University Press, 1961.

Nierenberg, Gerard, and Henry Calero. *How to Read a Person Like a Book.* New York: Hawthorn Books, 1971.

Ober, Richard L., Ernest L. Bentley, and Edith Miller. *Systematic Observation of Teaching: An Interaction Analysis—Instructional Strategy Approach.* Englewood Cliffs, N.J.: Prentice-Hall, 1971.

Sampson, Edward E. *Social Psychology and Contemporary Society.* New York: Wiley, 1971.

Sanders, Norris. *Classroom Questions: What Kinds?* New York: Harper & Row, 1966.

Scheflen, Albert. *Body Language and Social Order.* Englewood Cliffs, N.J.: Prentice-Hall, 1972.

Shuy, Roger. "Detroit Speech: Careless, Awkward, and Inconsistent, or Systematic, Graceful and Regular?" *Elementary English*, vol. 45, May 1968, pp. 565-69.

Smith, B. Othanel, and Milton O. Meux, in collaboration with Jerrold Coombs, Daniel Eierdam, and Ronald Szoke. *A Study of the Logic of Teaching.* U.S. Office of Education, Cooperative Research Project No. 258. Urbana, Ill.: Bureau of Educational Research, University of Illinois, 1962.

Sommer, Robert. *Personal Space: The Behavioral Basis of Design.* Englewood Cliffs, N.J.: Prentice-Hall, 1969.

Sommer, Robert. *Tight Spaces: Hard Architecture and How to Humanize It.* Englewood Cliffs, N.J.: Prentice-Hall, 1974.

Taba, Hilda. *Thinking in Elementary School Children.* San Francisco: San Francisco State College, 1964.

Thompson, J. J. *Beyond Words: Nonverbal Communication in the Classroom.* New York: Citation Press, 1973.

Weitz, Shirley (ed.). *Nonverbal Communication: Readings with Commentary.* New York: Oxford University Press, 1974.

Wolfram, Walt. "The Nature of Nonstandard Dialect Divergence," *Elementary English*, vol. 47, May 1970, pp. 739-48.

Index